myBook 5

Authors and Advisors

Alma Flor Ada • Kylene Beers • F. Isabel Campoy
Joyce Armstrong Carroll • Nathan Clemens
Anne Cunningham • Martha C. Hougen
Elena Izquierdo • Carol Jago • Erik Palmer
Robert E. Probst • Shane Templeton • Julie Washington

Contributing Consultants

David Dockterman • Mindset Works®
Jill Eggleton

Printed in the U.S.A.

ISBN   978-1-328-59253-8

1 2 3 4 5 6 7 8 9 10   0690   27 26 25 24 23 22 21 20 19

4500752825   A B C D E F G

HMH |

my Book 5

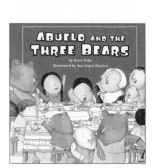

MODULE 10

Many Cultures, One World

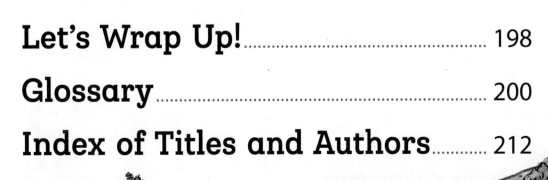

Home Sweet Habitat

"What is not good for the hive
is not good for the bee."

—Latin Proverb

How do living things in a habitat depend on each other?

Get Curious Video

Words About Animal Habitats

Complete the Vocabulary Network to show what you know about the words.

ecosystem

Meaning: An **ecosystem** is all the animals and plants that live in the same area.

Synonyms and Antonyms	Drawing

habitat

Meaning: A **habitat** is a place where plants and animals live and grow.

Synonyms and Antonyms	Drawing

species

Meaning: A **species** is a group of animals or plants that are alike.

Synonyms and Antonyms	Drawing

The Best Habitat for Me

An animal's habitat is the place where it lives. I'm a red panda, and my habitat is a cool, dark forest. In my opinion, it is the finest habitat in the world! The forest ecosystem has everything I need, so it is the best place for me to live.

A good habitat, like mine, should provide shelter. The forest has lots of trees. That is where I spend most of my time. The trees provide a place for me to sleep, especially during the hottest part of the day. Trees also keep me safe. The color of my fur helps me blend in with the trees so other animals can't see me as well. I can climb tall trees to escape if I am being chased.

This is me.

A good habitat should also provide food. Mostly, I eat bamboo. Many different species of bamboo grow in my habitat. I like to eat the shoots and leaves. Some of my other favorite foods are fruit, roots, and acorns. The insects I find on the ground are tasty, too.

ZZ ZZZ

Here I am taking a nap.

Bamboo leaves are yummy!

All animals need food and shelter. Some animals find these things in other habitats, like deserts or prairies. I have everything I need right here in the forest. Nothing is nicer than waking up in my favorite tree and knowing a tasty meal is close by. My forest home is the perfect home for me!

Home Sweet Home

It can be hard to see me in the trees.

Prepare to Read

GENRE STUDY **Informational text** is nonfiction. It gives facts about a topic. As you read *The Long, Long Journey*, pay attention to:

- order of events
- main topic and details
- how pictures and words help you understand the text

SET A PURPOSE **Ask questions** before, during, and after you read to help you get information or understand the text. Look for evidence in the text and pictures to **answer** your questions.

<table>
<tr><th colspan="1">POWER WORDS</th></tr>
<tr><td>wobbly</td></tr>
<tr><td>trills</td></tr>
<tr><td>crouches</td></tr>
<tr><td>coast</td></tr>
<tr><td>prances</td></tr>
<tr><td>flock</td></tr>
<tr><td>route</td></tr>
<tr><td>mingles</td></tr>
</table>

Meet Sandra Markle.

THE LONG, LONG JOURNEY

BY SANDRA MARKLE

ILLUSTRATED BY MIA POSADA

Crackle!
Crackle!
Crunch!

The little female bar-tailed godwit at last breaks free of her egg. She steps into the world on long, wobbly legs. It's nearly midnight, but it's June in Alaska and still light. A cool wind blows the chick's downy coat. She shivers, lifts her beak, and squeaks, "Peep! Peep!"

16

The little female was the last to hatch. Two sisters and a brother are nearby, with their father. They are hunting insects in the grass. Their mother next to the nest trills softly, and the chicks come running.

They huddle with their sister, and their mother settles over them. This way, the newest chick stays warm and joins the family.

For two days, the chicks stay close to the nest. Their parents take turns sitting on them to keep them warm. In between these rests, parents and chicks search for food. The parents need to double their body weight before fall. The chicks need to grow up and become strong.

The little female learns to hunt spiders, crane fly larvae, and beetles. She eats all she can find.

Soon the little godwit and her family wander farther as they feed. But they are rarely alone. Lots of other godwits nest and feed in this treeless land. Sometimes other hunters come searching for food too.

One day, an Arctic fox sneaks up and slips close to the little female.

19

But her father spots the fox and squawks a warning.

The little female is not yet able to fly. She crouches low and stays still. Her coloring helps her blend in with the grass. Her father flaps his wings and swoops at the fox.

Her mother joins the attack and so do other adult godwits. The fox runs off without its meal.

For almost a month, the female godwit chick eats and eats and grows bigger. She also grows feathers and loses her fluffy down coat.

When the chick isn't eating, she's hopping and flapping her wings. Her wings grow stronger with each hop-flap.

Then one day, the young female godwit
hops and flaps hard. For the first time,
she does what godwits do best.

She flies.

22

In mid-August, the mother godwit leaves. The young birds stay near their father. They eat and practice flying hour after hour so their wings grow even stronger. At last, they follow their father to the coast. They join thousands of godwits gathered on Alaska's Cape Avinof mudflats.

The young female prances across the mud on her long legs. Every step or two, she pokes her long beak deep into the muddy ground to find and eat tunneling worms and tiny clams.

In September, flock after flock of adult godwits leave the mudflats.

By mid-October, mostly only young birds remain. The young female is one of the flock. She practices flying with the other godwits. In between flights, she feeds alongside them. She eats and eats, growing very plump.

Finally, when dark clouds sweep overhead, the young female rises with the flock. She is pushed southward by strong winds. Her long journey has begun.

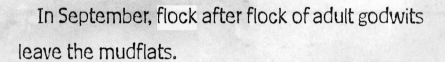

The young female flies
through unfamiliar skies
and over unknown seas.

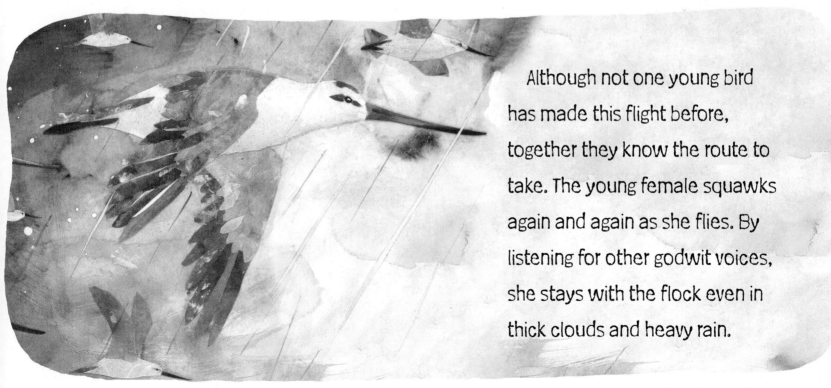

Although not one young bird
has made this flight before,
together they know the route to
take. The young female squawks
again and again as she flies. By
listening for other godwit voices,
she stays with the flock even in
thick clouds and heavy rain.

One day, a peregrine falcon hunting over an island swoops out of the clouds with wings folded and talon-tipped toes stretched out.

The falcon aims straight for the young female, but she pumps her wings hard, climbs fast, and escapes! Another godwit isn't so lucky.

Day after day and night after night, for nearly eight days, the godwits keep flying.

The young female is thin. Her wings stroke slower. Still, she keeps going.

Finally, there's green and brown ahead.

The young female swoops down with the flock to the New Zealand mudflats, where land mingles with the sea.

She arrives with two final wing flaps and lands on wobbly legs. Then folding her wings, she falls asleep.

The young female doesn't sleep for long, though. She needs to eat to get back her strength. She'll stay in New Zealand for two years until she's ready to raise a family of her own. Then, when March brings cool winds, she'll once again join the godwit flock and make the long, long journey back to Alaska.

Use details from *The Long, Long Journey* to answer these questions with a partner.

1. **Ask and Answer Questions** What questions did you ask yourself about the godwit before, during, and after reading? How did your questions help you understand the text?

2. Godwit chicks stay with their parents when they are young. How does this help them survive?

3. Using what you learned from the text, explain what it would be like to be a godwit chick.

Talking Tip

Listen carefully and politely. Say what you like about your partner's ideas.

Write a Travel Journal

PROMPT How would the young godwit describe her migration from Alaska to New Zealand? What does she see, hear, and feel? Use details from the text and illustrations to explain your ideas.

PLAN First, find details in the words and illustrations that show what the godwit sees, hears, and feels during her long journey. Add them to the chart.

Sees	Hears	Feels

WRITE Now write a travel journal entry from the godwit's point of view that tells about her journey. Remember to:

- Use the words *I* and *me* to describe the journey the way the godwit would.

- Describe the events of her journey in order.

_____

_____

_____

_____

_____

_____

_____

_____

_____

_____

Prepare to Read

GENRE STUDY **Informational text** is nonfiction. It gives facts about a topic.

MAKE A PREDICTION Preview "Wolves to the Rescue!" Ideas about wolves have changed over the years. What do you think you will learn from reading this text?

_____

_____

_____

_____

_____

_____

SET A PURPOSE Read to find out how wolves can be an important part of a natural habitat.

Wolves to the Rescue!

READ What events caused other events to happen?

Once, gray wolves were not welcome in the United States. Farmers said the wolves were killing their animals, so people killed wolves to protect the animals. By 1926, no wolves were left in Yellowstone National Park, a large park in the states of Wyoming, Montana, and Idaho. Then scientists realized how important wolves had been to the park. The wolves hunted elk for food. Without wolves, the number of elk grew and grew. ▶

Close Reading Tip

Put a ? by the parts you have questions about.

CHECK MY UNDERSTANDING

What caused the number of elk in Yellowstone to grow?

_____

_____

READ What happened next in the park?

Close Reading Tip

<u>Underline</u> words the author uses to help you understand the order of events.

The elk liked to eat willow trees. That led to a problem. Beavers use willow trees to build dams across rivers. The dams make ponds. Without willow, beavers stopped building dams. Ponds dried up. Fish and reptiles had fewer places to live.

Scientists said bringing the wolves back would help solve this problem. People listened. In 1995 and 1996, 31 wolves were brought to Yellowstone. After that, there were fewer elk to eat willow trees, and beavers built dams again. The dams formed ponds where fish and reptiles could make their homes.

Today, there are more than 108 wolves in Yellowstone.

CHECK MY UNDERSTANDING

What questions did you ask yourself before, during, and after reading? How did your questions help you understand the text?

_____

_____

_____

WRITE ABOUT IT Do you think bringing wolves back to Yellowstone was a good idea? Use details from the text to explain your opinion.

_____

_____

_____

_____

_____

_____

_____

_____

_____

_____

Prepare to Read

GENRE STUDY **Informational text** is nonfiction. It gives facts about a topic. As you read *Sea Otter Pups,* pay attention to:

- details and facts about a topic
- maps that help explain a topic
- pictures with labels

SET A PURPOSE As you read, stop and think if you don't understand something. Reread, ask yourself questions, use what you already know, and look for visual clues to help you understand the text.

POWER WORDS

surface

wraps

attached

crack

Build Background: Ocean Habitat

Sea Otter Pups

by Ruth Owen

Meet a sea otter pup

A mother sea otter and her pup are floating in the ocean. The mother otter is resting on her back. The little pup is cuddled up on his mother's belly, just above the water.

mother sea otter

sea otter pup

What is a sea otter?

Sea otters are animals that live in the ocean. They are about as big as a medium-size dog. Sea otters have very thick fur. The fur helps keep the otter's body warm and dry in the cold water.

Adult sea otter size

adult sea otter

thick fur

Where do sea otters live?

Although sea otters live in the ocean, they stay close to the shore. The yellow parts of this map show where sea otters live.

shore

sea otters

Russia

Alaska

Canada

Pacific Ocean

N
W E
S

United States

Japan

Where sea otters live

A newborn pup

A mother sea otter gives birth in the ocean to just one pup at a time. After the pup is born, she places it on her chest to keep it warm. Then she feeds it milk from her body. A pup drinks its mother's milk until it's about four to six months old.

41

Learning to swim

A newborn sea otter cannot swim, but it can float really well. It floats on top of the water like a beach ball! The mother sea otter gives her pup swimming lessons. By the time it is about 14 weeks old, the pup is able to swim and dive.

floating mother sea otter

floating pup

Sea otter food

Sea otter adults and pups eat crabs, clams, and other shellfish. The mother otter dives under the water to hunt for food. She teaches the pup how to dive and find shellfish, too.

clam

mother otter

crab

pup

43

Time for dinner

Once the mother sea otter finds a clam, she swims back up to the water's surface. She also brings a rock with her and lays it on her belly. Then she smashes the clam onto the rock to open its shell. The mother otter and the pup share the clam meat.

clam

sea otter pup

mother otter

clam meat

44

sleeping adult
sea otter

kelp

Goodnight!

When it is time to sleep, an adult sea otter sometimes wraps seaweed around its body. The seaweed, called kelp, is attached to the ocean floor. It holds the otter in one place. This keeps the waves from carrying the otter out into the ocean. Sometimes the mother otter also wraps kelp around the pup as it sleeps on her chest.

45

Growing up

When a pup is between 6 and 12 months old, it leaves its mother. It knows how to dive underwater to hunt for food. It can use rocks to crack open shellfish. The pup is now ready to begin its grown-up life!

Turn and Talk

Use details from *Sea Otter Pups* to answer these questions with a partner.

1. **Monitor and Clarify** What did you do when you came to a part of the text that you didn't understand? Tell how it helped or didn't help you.

2. Which details in the text help you figure out the topic and central idea?

3. Compare the animal habitats in *Sea Otter Pups* and *The Long, Long Journey*. How do the habitats meet the animals' needs?

Talking Tip

Answer your partner's questions. Explain your ideas clearly.

I mean that _____.

Write a Description

PROMPT Imagine that you are a scientist observing a mother sea otter and her pup in their habitat. Describe what you see and hear. Use details from the text and photographs to help you.

PLAN First, make notes about what the habitat is like. Next, make notes about the sea otters. What do they look like? What are they doing?

Habitat	Sea Otters

WRITE Now write a description of a mother sea otter and her pup in their habitat. Remember to:

- Use exact adjectives to describe the otters and their habitat.

- Include details that show how the habitat helps them survive.

_____

_____

_____

_____

_____

_____

_____

_____

_____

_____

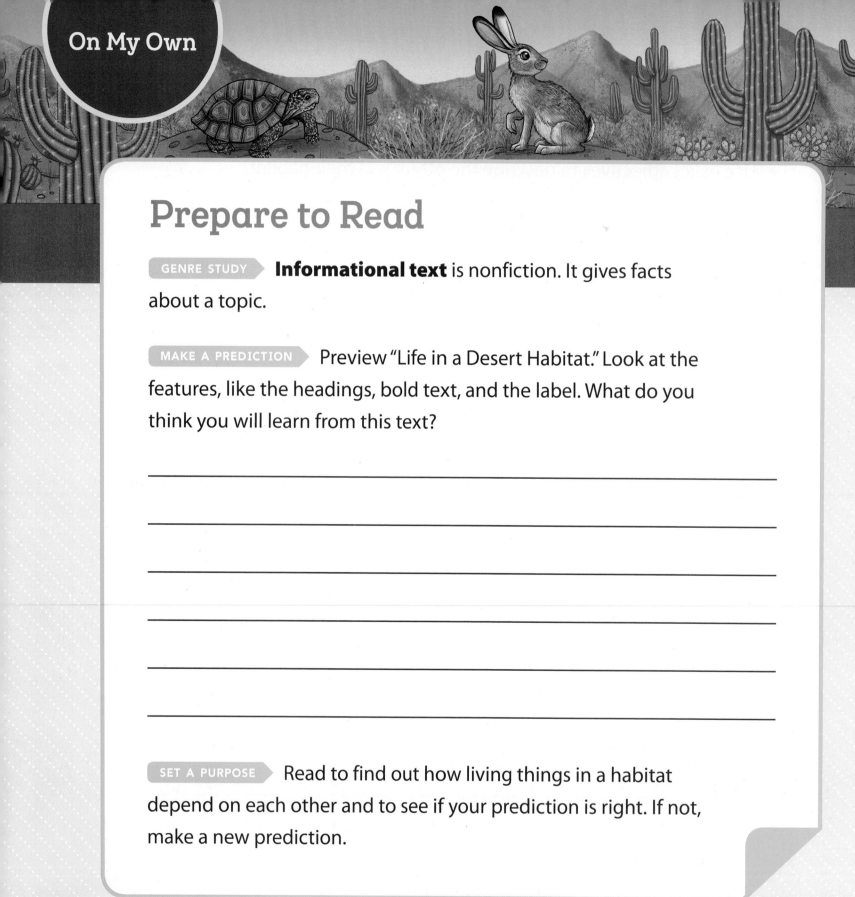

Prepare to Read

GENRE STUDY **Informational text** is nonfiction. It gives facts about a topic.

MAKE A PREDICTION Preview "Life in a Desert Habitat." Look at the features, like the headings, bold text, and the label. What do you think you will learn from this text?

_____

_____

_____

_____

_____

_____

SET A PURPOSE Read to find out how living things in a habitat depend on each other and to see if your prediction is right. If not, make a new prediction.

saguaro cactus

Life in a Desert Habitat

READ What is the central idea of this part of the text?

What Is a Desert Habitat?

A desert is one kind of habitat. It is a dry place with little rain. Some deserts are hot, while others are cold. The living things in a desert depend on each other. Some animals, such as desert tortoises, eat plants for food. Animals that eat other animals for food, such as coyotes, are called **predators**. The animals that predators hunt are called **prey**. ▶

Close Reading Tip

<u>Underline</u> the heading and the label. Did they help you make a correct prediction? What was different?

CHECK MY UNDERSTANDING

How do the picture and label help you understand the text?

_____

_____

_____

51

Animals Protect Themselves

Prey animals protect themselves from predators in different ways. The desert tortoise has a hard shell that protects it. The tortoise can pull its head and legs into the shell if a predator is nearby. An elf owl stays safe by making its nest high up in a cactus where most predators can't reach.

Some animals, such as the jackrabbit, have **camouflage** to stay safe. The colors and markings on their bodies help them blend into their surroundings. Jackrabbits also use their strong back legs to run fast and escape predators. They can reach speeds up to 40 miles per hour! That is as fast as the speed limit for cars on some roads.

Close Reading Tip

Underline words that help you figure out what the word *camouflage* means.

CHECK MY UNDERSTANDING

What did you do when you came to a part of the text that you didn't understand? Tell how it did or didn't help you.

_____

_____

WRITE ABOUT IT Describe how plants and animals in a desert depend on each other. Include details and words you learned from the text in your answer.

_____

_____

_____

_____

_____

_____

_____

_____

_____

_____

Prepare to Read

GENRE STUDY **Poetry** uses images, sounds, and rhythm to express feelings. As you read the poems in *At Home in the Wild*, pay attention to:

- repetition of words or lines
- words that describe
- rhythm, or beats, between words

SET A PURPOSE As you read, **create mental images,** or make pictures in your mind, to help you understand details in the text.

POWER WORDS
sheltered
weary
hide
wit

Build Background: Animal Homes

At Home in the Wild

Poetry and Song

Polar Bear Family

by Eileen Spinelli

Polar bear mama moves with grace
to find a sheltered winter place.
She digs a snow cave wide and deep
where she and baby cubs can sleep.

Come spring, the cubs set out for fun.
They romp all day in the Arctic sun.
They slip and slide. They race and roam.
Then, weary, ride their mama home.

Big Brown Moose

by Joyce Sidman

I'm a big brown moose,
I'm a rascally moose,
I'm a moose with a tough, shaggy hide;
and I kick and I prance
in a long-legged dance
with my moose-mama close by my side.

I shrug off the cold
and I sneeze at the wind
and I swivel my ears in the snow;
and I tramp and I tromp
over forest and swamp,
'cause there's nowhere a moose cannot go.

I'm a big brown moose,
I'm a ravenous moose
as I hunt for the willow and yew;
with a snort and a crunch,
I rip off each bunch,
and I chew and I chew and I chew.

58

When together we slump
in a comfortable clump—
my mountainous mama and I—
I give her a nuzzle
of velvety muzzle.
Our frosty breath drifts to the sky.

I'm a big brown moose,
I'm a slumberous moose,
I'm a moose with a warm, snuggly hide;
and I bask in the moon
as the coyotes croon,
with my moose-mama close by my side.

59

Over in the Meadow

1. O-ver in the mea-dow, in the sand, in the sun,

Lived a sweet moth-er frog and her lit-tle frog-gie one.

"Croak!" said the mo-ther; "I croak," said the one, So

they croaked and they croaked in the sand, in the sun.

2. Over in the meadow, in the stream so blue,
   Lived a shiny mother fish and her little fishies two.
   "Swim!" said the mother; "We swim," said the two,
   So they swam and they swam in the stream so blue.

3. Over in the meadow, on a branch of the tree,
   Lived a wise mother bird and her little birdies three.
   "Sing!" said the mother; "We sing," said the three,
   So they sang and they sang on a branch of the tree.

4. Over in the meadow, at a den near the shore,
   Lived a mighty mother wolf and her little cubs four.
   "Howl!" said the mother; "We howl," said the four,
   So they howled and they howled at their den near the shore.

5. Over in the meadow, in a busy beehive,
   Lived a fuzzy mother bee and her little bees five.
   "Buzz!" said the mother; "We buzz," said the five,
   So they buzzed and they buzzed in a busy beehive.

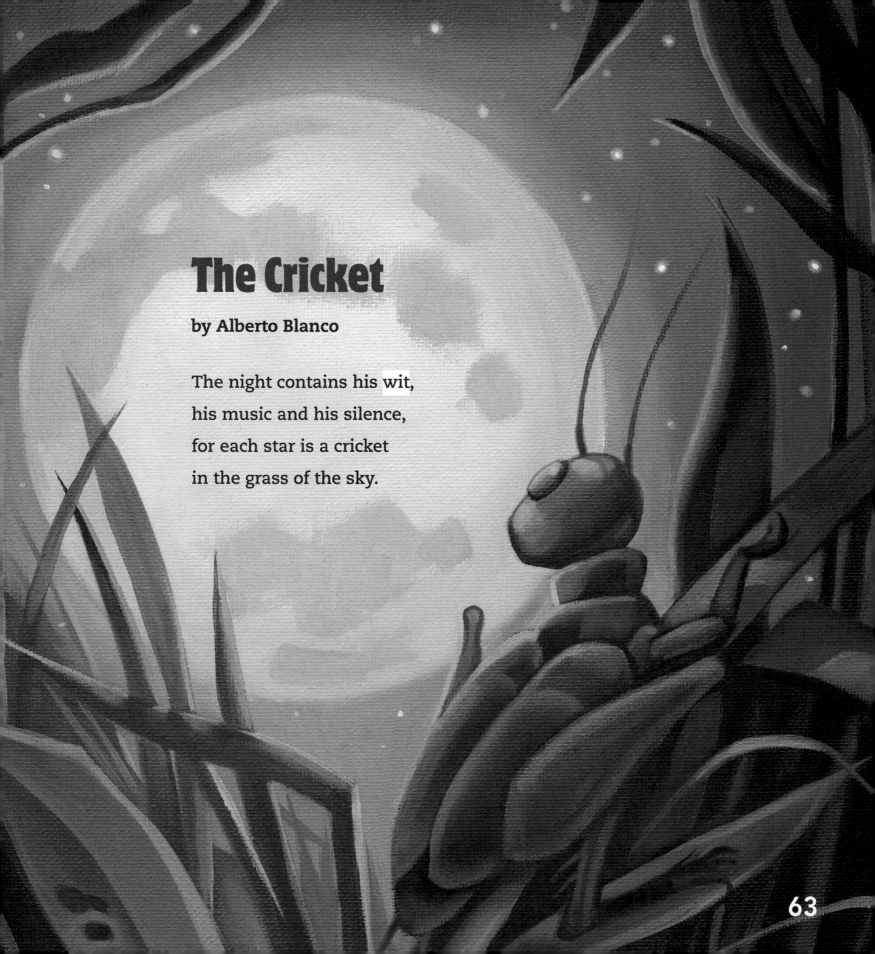

The Cricket

by Alberto Blanco

The night contains his wit,
his music and his silence,
for each star is a cricket
in the grass of the sky.

The Ant

by Alma Flor Ada
and F. Isabel Campoy

Here comes the ant
Out of its hole,
Grabs a grain of wheat
And returns like a mole.

Another ant comes
Out of its hole,
Grabs a grain of wheat
And returns like a mole.

ANOTHER ant comes
Out of its hole . . .

Turn and Talk

Use details from *At Home in the Wild* to answer these questions with a partner.

1. **Create Mental Images** Close your eyes. Picture walking in a habitat in one of the poems. What would you see, hear, and feel? Which of the poet's words help you create the picture?

2. If "The Ant" were longer, what would the next line be? Why do you think the poet uses repetition in this poem?

3. How do the poems make you feel? How do the poets use rhythm and rhyme to create those feelings?

Talking Tip

Ask to learn more about your partner's ideas.

Please explain _____.

Write a Song

PROMPT How could you change "Over in the Meadow" to make it about a different animal habitat? Look carefully at the song. Notice the rhyme pattern and repetition. Which words would you need to change to describe another habitat?

PLAN First, choose the habitat you will write about. On one side of the chart, list animals that live there. On the other side, list the sounds the animals make.

Animals	Animal Sounds

WRITE Now change the words in "Over in the Meadow" to write your own animal habitats song! Remember to:

- Include details that tell what the animal habitat is like.

- Use words that fit the rhyming pattern of the song.

_____

_____

_____

_____

_____

_____

_____

_____

_____

_____

Prepare to Read

Poetry uses images, sounds, and rhythm to express feelings.

Preview the poems, "Pond in Summer" and "Pond in Winter." A poet describes a pond in different seasons. How do you think these two poems will be different?

_____

_____

_____

_____

_____

_____

Read to see how the poet uses words to paint two very different pictures of a pond.

Picture a Pond

READ What do you picture when you read this poem?

Pond in Summer

A summer pond is a busy place,

Everything moves at a faster pace,

Water lilies open their flowers,

Fragrant in the morning hours,

While crawly creatures take a ride,

On the lilies' other side.

A summer pond is a busy place,

Everything moves at a faster pace.

Close Reading Tip

<u>Underline</u> words that rhyme.

CHECK MY UNDERSTANDING

Why do you think the poet repeats lines in the poem?

_____

_____

69

READ How is the way you picture the pond different when you read this poem?

Pond in Winter

Frozen pond,

Blanket of snow,

Little sunlight,

Food supply low.

Some animals sleep,

When there's nothing to eat.

And the pond's turned into

An icy sheet.

Close Reading Tip

Underline the words that help you picture the pond in winter.

CHECK MY UNDERSTANDING

Why do you think the poet wrote this poem using short lines?

_____

_____

_____

_____

_____

_____

WRITE ABOUT IT Which of the two poems is your favorite?
Use details to explain why.

_____

_____

_____

_____

_____

_____

_____

_____

_____

_____

_____

Prepare to Read

GENRE STUDY **Folktales** are old tales passed down over time through storytelling. When you read *Abuelo and the Three Bears,* look for:

- animal characters that act and talk like people
- author's purpose (to entertain or explain?)
- the beginning, middle, and ending of the story
- how pictures and words help you understand what happens

SET A PURPOSE As you read, **retell** the story. Use your own words to tell what happened in the beginning, middle, and end of the story.

POWER WORDS

arrive

grumpy

joking

tucked

stubborn

growled

shrugged

offered

Build Background: Bears

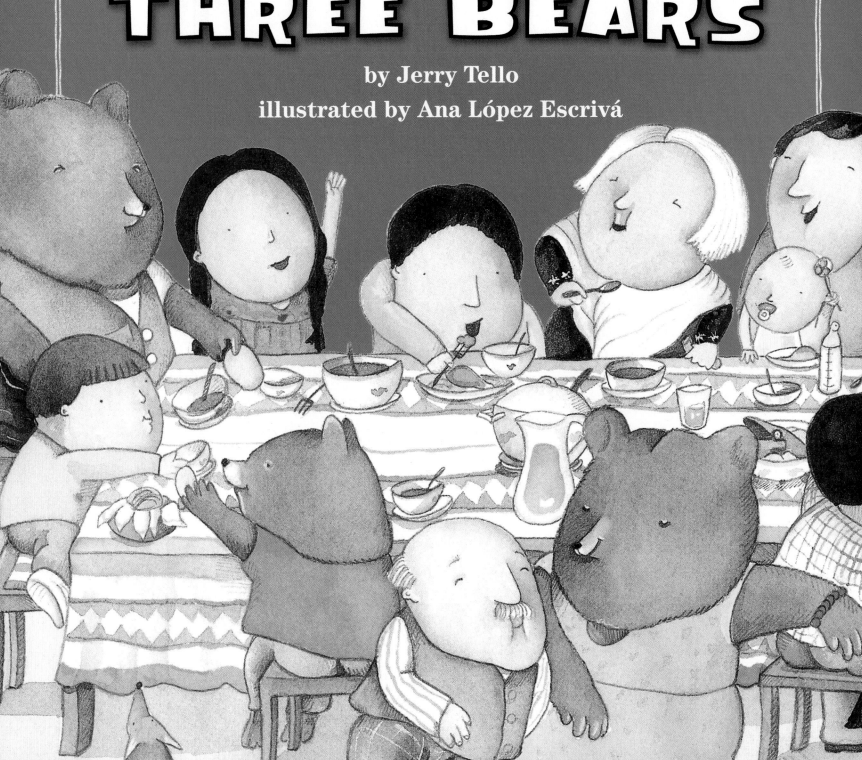

ABUELO AND THE THREE BEARS

by Jerry Tello

illustrated by Ana López Escrivá

It was a quiet Sunday. Emilio and his grandfather sat on the front porch.

"Abuelo," said Emilio, "do we have to wait much longer? When will everybody get here?"

"Your cousins will arrive soon," Abuelo answered, "and we'll have a fine dinner. I'll tell you a story to help pass the time."

Once there were three bears who lived in the woods—Papá Bear, Mamá Bear, and their little Osito. One Sunday morning, Papá Bear woke up as grumpy as ever. Then he smelled something good. "Mmmm, frijoles!" he said.

"Abuelo, you're joking!" laughed Emilio. "Bears don't like beans!"

"Well, all the bears I know like frijoles," said Abuelo.

Papá Bear got up and rushed down to the kitchen.
"Buenos días," said Papá Bear to Mamá Bear and Osito.

Papá Bear sat down at the table and tucked a napkin under his chin. "How are the frijoles? Are they ready yet?" he asked. "Yes," answered Mamá Bear, "but they're still too hot to eat."

"I can't wait," said Papá Bear. "I'm so hungry I could eat an elephant."

"Abuelo," said Emilio, "bears don't eat elephants."

"Emilio," answered Abuelo, "you must never argue with a hungry bear."

77

Stubborn Papá Bear didn't listen to Mamá Bear's warning.

"¡Ay!" he growled, jumping out of his chair. "These beans are too hot!"

"I told you so," said Mamá Bear. "Why don't we take a walk into town while they cool?"

"All right," grumbled Papá Bear, whose mouth was still burning. So the bears left their breakfast to cool and went out.

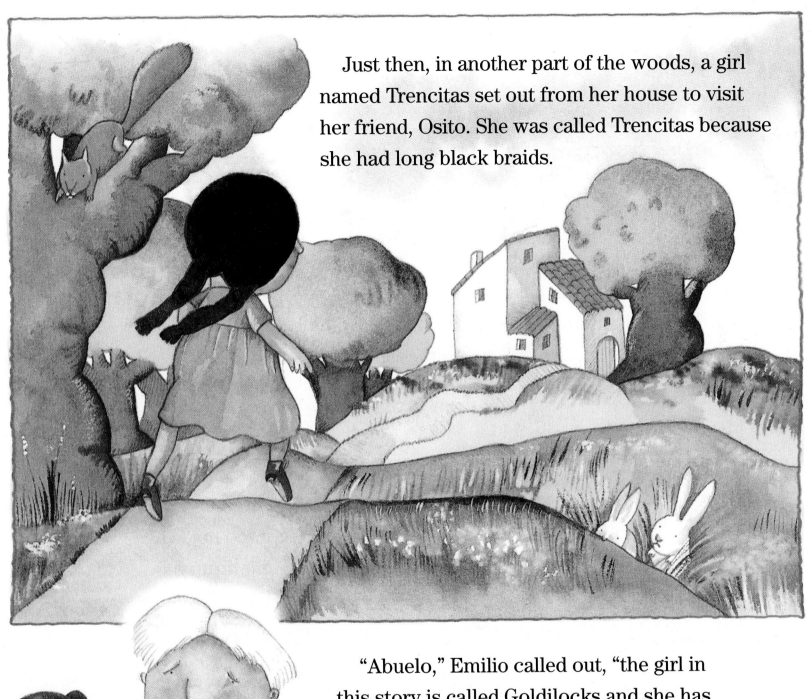

Just then, in another part of the woods, a girl named Trencitas set out from her house to visit her friend, Osito. She was called Trencitas because she had long black braids.

"Abuelo," Emilio called out, "the girl in this story is called Goldilocks and she has blond hair."

"Goldilocks?" Abuelo shrugged. "In my story it was Trencitas with her long black braids who came to visit. And she was hungry, too!"

79

When Trencitas arrived at Osito's house, she noticed that the door was open. So she stepped inside and followed her nose until she came to the three bowls of beans.

First Trencitas tasted some beans from the great big bowl, but they were too hot. Then she tasted some from the medium-sized bowl, but they were too cold. Finally she tasted some from the little bowl, and they were just right. So she finished them all up.

Now Trencitas decided to sit in the living room and wait for the bears to return. She sat in the great big chair, but it was too hard. She sat in the medium-sized chair, but it was too soft. Then she sat in the little chair, and it was just right until . . . CRASH!

"Abuelo, what's Trencitas going to do?" asked Emilio. "She broke her friend's chair."

"Don't worry," Abuelo said. "She'll come back later with glue and leave it like new."

Trencitas was feeling very sleepy. She went upstairs to take a rest. First she tried the great big bed, but the blanket was scratchy. Then she tried the medium-sized bed, but it was too lumpy. Finally she tried the little bed. It was too small, but it was so cozy and soft that Trencitas soon fell asleep.

When the three bears came home, Papá Bear headed straight to the kitchen to eat his frijoles.

"¡Ay!" he growled when he saw his bowl. "Somebody's been eating my beans."

"And somebody's been eating my beans," said Mamá Bear.

"And there's only one bean left in my bowl," said Osito.

Then the three bears went into the living room.

"¡Ay!" said Papá Bear, when he saw that his chair had been moved. "Somebody's been sitting in my chair."

"And somebody's been sitting in my chair," said Mamá Bear.

"And my chair is all over the place!" said Osito.

The three bears climbed the stairs to check out the bedrooms. Papá Bear went first. Mamá Bear and Osito followed behind him.

"¡Ay!" said Papá Bear, when he looked in the bedroom. "Somebody's been sleeping in my bed."

"And somebody's been sleeping in my bed," said Mamá Bear.

"Look who's sleeping in my bed!" said Osito. He ran over to Trencitas and woke her up. Then they all had a good laugh.

By now it was getting late. Mamá Bear said they'd walk Trencitas home to make sure she got there safely.

Papá Bear did not like this idea. "Another walk!" he growled. "What about my frijoles?"

"There'll be beans at my house," offered Trencitas.

"I'll bet that made Papá Bear happy," said Emilio.

"You're right," said Abuelo. "Here's what happened next . . . ."

When they all arrived at Trencitas's house, they sat down at a long table with Trencitas's parents, grandparents, uncles, aunts, and lots of cousins. They ate pork and fish and chicken and tortillas and beans and salsa so hot it brought tears to their eyes. And they laughed and shared stories.

"So you see, Emilio," said Abuelo, "Papá Bear had to wait a long time to eat his frijoles. But, in the end, he had a wonderful meal and lots of fun, just as you will when your cousins arrive."

"Is that the end of the story?" Emilio asked.

"Yes," answered Abuelo, "and it's the end of your waiting, too!"

GLOSSARY	
Abuelo	Grandfather
Osito	Little Bear
Frijoles	Beans
Buenos días	Good morning
¡Ay!	Oh!
Trencitas	Little Braids
Tortillas	Thin corn pancakes
Salsa	Spicy tomato and chile dip

Use details from *Abuelo and the Three Bears* to answer these questions with a partner.

1. **Retell** Take turns telling the story events in order. Use order words such as *first, next, after,* and *at the end* to help you.

2. Who is telling the story? How would the story be different if one of the three bears were telling it?

3. How is this story like another story you know? How is it different? Compare the characters, setting, and events in both stories.

Talking Tip

Be polite. Wait for your turn to talk. Then tell your idea to your partner.

I think that _____.

Write a Drama

PROMPT Imagine you wake up at the three bears' house. What happens next? Write a short drama to tell what happens. Look back at the text and illustrations for ideas.

PLAN First, draw or write what will happen first, next, and last in your drama.

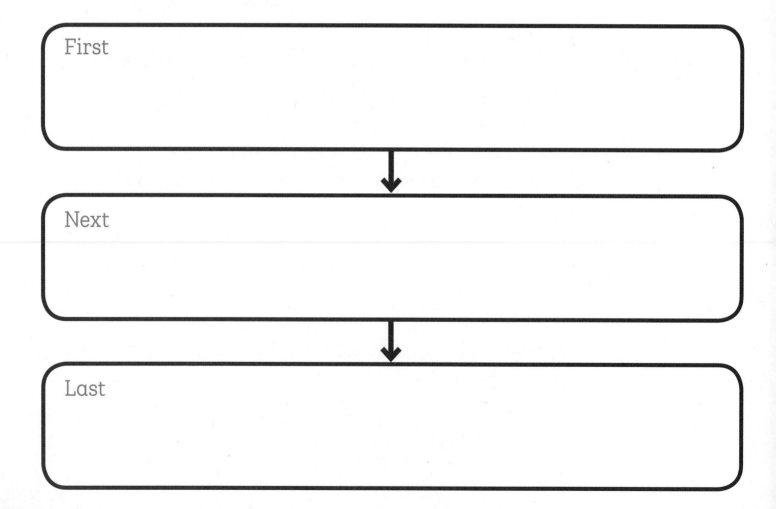

First

Next

Last

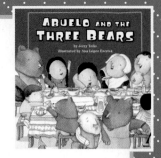

WRITE Now write your drama. Include details in the dialogue that bring your characters to life. Remember to:

- Name the **characters** and the **setting.**

- Include **stage directions** to show what the characters are feeling or doing.

- Include a **narrator** to help describe the action.

_____

_____

_____

_____

_____

_____

_____

_____

_____

Prepare to Read

GENRE STUDY **Folktales** are old tales passed down over time through storytelling.

MAKE A PREDICTION Preview "The Story of Crocodile and Hen." A hen crosses paths with a very hungry crocodile. What do you think will happen?

_____

_____

_____

_____

_____

_____

_____

SET A PURPOSE Read to find out what happens when Crocodile and Hen meet.

The Story of Crocodile and Hen

READ What happens at the beginning of the folktale?

One day, Crocodile felt hungry enough to eat a whole forest. He waited in the river for Hen to stop by for a drink.

"I am going to eat you!" Crocodile snarled at Hen, flashing a big set of teeth as sharp as nails.

"Don't eat me, brother!" Hen replied calmly. Then she coolly walked away as Crocodile stared after her with surprise. ▶

Close Reading Tip

<u>Underline</u> words that show how Hen and Crocodile are feeling.

CHECK MY UNDERSTANDING

Why does the author say Crocodile was "hungry enough to eat a whole forest"? Does Crocodile want to eat the forest?

_____

_____

_____

Close Reading Tip

<u>Underline</u> words that Crocodile repeats. Why does he repeat those words?

"Brother? Me? Brother?" Crocodile stammered as he watched Hen go. "What is that chicken talking about?"

"Of course you're her brother!" his friend Lizard cried.

Crocodile was completely stunned. "But—but—that's impossible! I have green shiny skin, and she has fluffy white feathers—we are just not alike in any way!"

"Nonsense," Lizard said, with a toss of her tail. "Hens lay eggs, don't they? Crocodiles do, too, right?"

Crocodile thought for a moment. "You make a good point. We must be related. I have a sister! I am a brother!"

"Now you get the picture!" exclaimed Lizard.

"I guess I won't eat her then," said Crocodile with a smile.

CHECK MY UNDERSTANDING

What does Lizard mean when she says, "Now you get the picture!"?

_____

_____

WRITE ABOUT IT Retell "The Story of Crocodile and Hen."
Describe the characters and events in your own words.

_____

_____

_____

_____

_____

_____

_____

_____

_____

_____

_____

Prepare to View

GENRE STUDY **Videos** are short movies that give you
information or something for you to watch for enjoyment. As
you watch *Ducklings Jump from Nest,* notice:

- how pictures, sounds, and words work together
- what the video is about
- information about the topic
- the tone or mood of the video

SET A PURPOSE One way that events can be told is in
chronological order. That means they are told in the order they
happened. Pay attention to the order of events in the video. How
does the order help you understand how the events are related?

Build Background: Nests

DUCKLINGS JUMP
FROM NEST

by Terra Mater Factual Studios

As You View These little ducklings are about to have a big adventure! As you watch, think about the order of events in the video. Pay attention to how the visuals, words, and sounds help you understand what it is like to be inside the ducklings' nest.

Use details from *Ducklings Jump from Nest* to answer these questions with a partner.

1. **Chronological Order** What do the ducklings do while their mom is in the nest? What do they do after she jumps out of the nest?

2. What does the narrator mean when he says, "some ducklings aren't as bold as others"?

3. How does the video make you feel? How do the narrator's words and the music help to make you feel that way?

Listening Tip

Listen carefully. Think about the meaning of what your partner says.

Let's Wrap Up!

 **Essential Question**

How do living things in a habitat depend on each other?

··

Pick one of these activities to show what you have learned about the topic.

1. Imagine That! Story

Choose an animal habitat you read about. Imagine that the whole world is made up of that habitat. How would it change the way some animals and people live? Write a story that tells what it would be like. Include details you learned from the texts.

2. Habitat Trivia

Work with a partner. Write three questions about the habitats you read about. Be sure that the answers are in one of the texts you read. Then, play habitat trivia in a group. Challenge each other to answer your habitat questions.

Word Challenge

Can you use the word species in one of your questions?

My Notes

Many Cultures, One World

"We are all the same and we are all different.
What great friends we will be."

—Kelly Moran

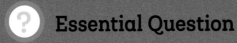
What can we learn from different people and cultures?

Get Curious
Video

Words About World Cultures

Complete the Vocabulary Network to show what you know about the words.

culture

Meaning: A group's **culture** is the ideas and beliefs the people share.

Synonyms and Antonyms	Drawing

harmony

Meaning: Being in **harmony** means living together in a peaceful way.

Synonyms and Antonyms	Drawing

heritage

Meaning: A country's **heritage** is its way of doing things that is passed down over time.

Synonyms and Antonyms	Drawing

Hello, World!

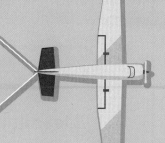

If you took a trip around the world, you would learn about different cultures and traditions. You would meet different people, taste different foods, and hear different kinds of music. You would also hear different languages.

Germany

China

Kenya

Argentina

Every country has special ways of saying *hello*, *goodbye*, and *thank you*.

Understanding different languages and traditions helps us live in harmony. What traditions are part of your heritage?

106

Argentina

¡Hola!

guau guau!

hello = hola (OH-lah)
goodbye = chau (CHOW)
thank you = gracias (GRAH-see-us)

China

Nĭ hăo!

wang wang

hello = nĭ hăo (nee-HOW)
goodbye = zài jiàn (ZYE-chin)
thank you = xiè xiè (SYEH-syeh)

Kenya

Jambo!

woef woef

hello = jambo (JAHM-boh)
goodbye = kwaheri (kwah-HEH-ree)
thank you = asante (uh-SAHN-tay)

Germany

Hallo!

wuff wuff

hello = hallo (HAH-low)
goodbye = auf wiedersehen
            (OWF VEE-dur-zayn)
thank you = danke (DAHN-kuh)

Prepare to Read

GENRE STUDY **Realistic fiction** stories are made up but could happen in real life. When you read *Where on Earth Is My Bagel?*, look for:

- characters that act and talk like real people
- problems and solutions
- ways pictures and words help readers understand the story

SET A PURPOSE Read to make smart guesses, or **inferences,** about things the author does not say. Use clues in the text and pictures to help you.

POWER WORDS
darting
smothered
nod
slippery
hollered
delight
fragrant
grunted

Meet Grace Lin.

Where on Earth
Is My Bagel?

by Frances Park and
Ginger Park

illustrated by Grace Lin

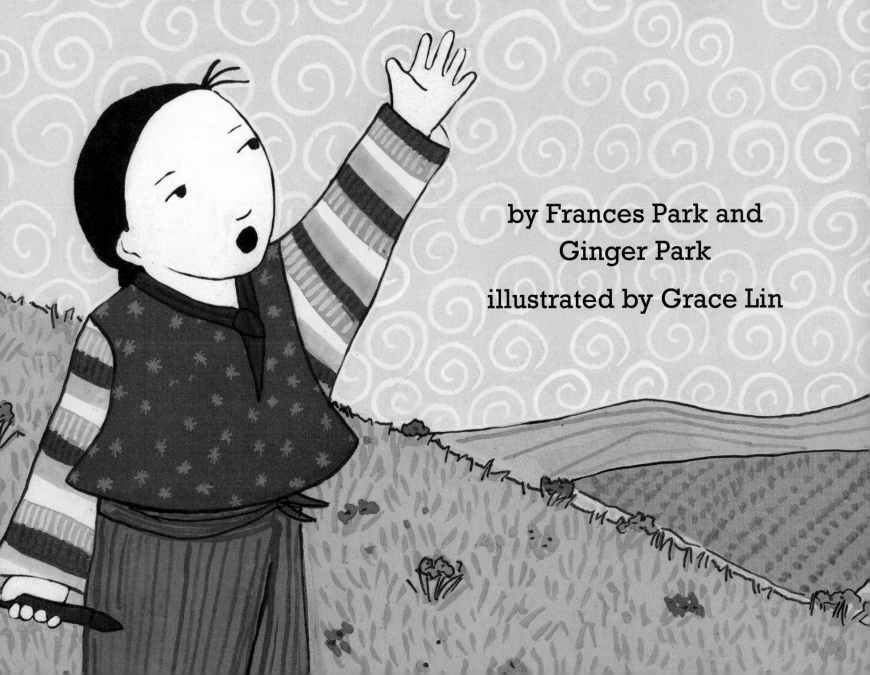

Once there was a boy named Yum Yung who lived in a village where the mountains met the sky. There were waterfalls rushing into streams of darting fish. There were lilacs gently blossoming on every hillside.

But there were no New York bagels!

110

How a New York bagel popped into Yum Yung's head was a mystery. Perhaps it came to him in a dream, smothered with cream cheese. Or maybe he heard sparrows singing of bagel crumbs in Central Park.

However it happened, Yum Yung could not stop thinking about a golden brown bagel with a curious hole in the middle. The very idea made his tummy growl and his mouth water.

Yum Yung declared:

"I want a bagel!"

Now dreaming about a New York bagel and actually eating a New York bagel were worlds apart.

Yum Yung wondered, "Where can I find a bagel?" He wondered and wondered, until he came up with an idea. "I will send a message!" he said.

So he sat on a rock and began to write:

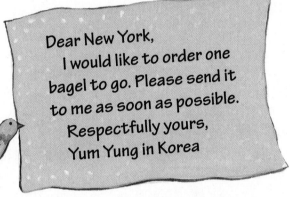

Dear New York,
    I would like to order one bagel to go. Please send it to me as soon as possible.
        Respectfully yours,
        Yum Yung in Korea

Yum Yung carried his message to a mountaintop where birds flocked. Soon a pigeon landed on his shoulder. Yum Yung tied his message to the bird's tiny leg and the pigeon flew off into the clouds.

"Pigeon," he cried out, "please return with my bagel!"

Yum Yung waited and waited on the
mountaintop. He waited until the sun dipped
below the mountain. He waited until the sky was
blanketed with stars. But the pigeon did not return
with his New York bagel.

Yum Yung decided that his bagel must be lost. Perhaps
the pigeon dropped his bagel on the wrong mountaintop.
Or maybe it was delivered to the wrong person.

However it happened, Yum Yung would not give up hope.
A search was in order!

Yum Yung declared:

"Where on Earth is my bagel?"

The next morning Yum Yung visited Farmer
Ahn, who was pushing his plow in a field of wheat.

"Excuse me, Farmer Ahn," Yum Yung said.
"Have you seen my missing bagel?"

Farmer Ahn wiped the sweat off his forehead.
"Bagel? What in a farmer's field is a bagel?"

114

"It is round and it has a hole in the middle," Yum Yung explained.

"Hmm," Farmer Ahn said with a nod. He pointed to his plow wheel. "Is that a bagel?"

Yum Yung frowned. "No, that is not my bagel."

"I am sorry, Yum Yung," Farmer Ahn said. "I know about wheat that grows from the rich brown earth, but I know nothing about bagels."

Next Yum Yung visited Fisherman Kee, who was on his boat shaking slippery fish out of his net.

"Excuse me, Fisherman Kee," Yum Yung shouted. "Have you seen my missing bagel?"

Fisherman Kee threw his net back into the water with a splash. "Bagel? What in the salty sea is a bagel?"

"It is round and it has a hole in the middle," Yum Yung explained.

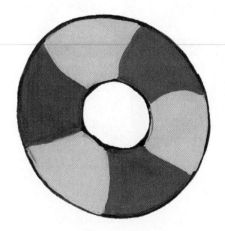

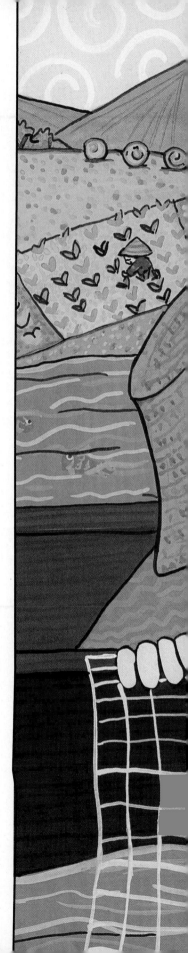

"Oh," Fisherman Kee said with a nod. He pointed to his life ring floating below. "Is that a bagel?"

Yum Yung frowned. "No, that is not my bagel."

"I am sorry, Yum Yung," Fisherman Kee said. "I know about fish that swim in the sea, but I know nothing about bagels."

Next Yum Yung visited Beekeeper Lee, who was collecting honey from a beehive.

"Excuse me, Beekeeper Lee," Yum Yung hollered from a distance. "Have you seen my missing bagel?"

Beekeeper Lee raised her bee veil. "Bagel? What in the sweet name of honey is a bagel?"

"It is round and it has a hole in the middle," Yum Yung explained.

"Ah," Beekeeper Lee said with a nod. She pointed to the thick swarm of bees circling over her head. "Is that a bagel?"

Yum Yung frowned. "No, that is not my bagel."

"I am sorry, Yum Yung," Beekeeper Lee said. "I know about the buzzing business of bees, but I know nothing about bagels."

Yum Yung sat down on a quiet hillside and moaned. All hope for a bagel seemed lost!

Then a delicious smell tickled his nose. He sniffed curiously. Where was it coming from?

Yum Yung looked into the valley and blinked with delight.

There was Oh's Heavenly Bakery!

119

Yum Yung rushed into Oh's Heavenly Bakery, where Baker Oh was making one of her famous rice cakes.

"Baker Oh," Yum Yung pleaded, "please tell me you have my missing bagel!"

Baker Oh sprinkled a few pine nuts on the rice cake. "Bagel? What in a baker's kitchen is a bagel?"

"It is round, and it has a hole in the middle," Yum Yung explained.

"I am very sorry, Yum Yung," Baker Oh said. "I have not seen your missing bagel. But maybe that pigeon tapping at the window has better news for you."

Baker Oh opened the window. The bird flew in and landed on Yum Yung's shoulder—with a message!

While Baker Oh fed the pigeon rice cake crumbs, Yum Yung read the message aloud.

Dear Yum Yung,

Thanks a million for your order of one bagel to go. I'm real sorry, but my bagels only stay fresh on the same day they're made. So I'll do the next best thing and send you the secret recipe for my number one New York bagel!

Good luck!

Joe

From Joe's To-Go Bagels

P.S.
recipe on other side

Baker Oh studied the recipe, then frowned.

"I am afraid I do not have all the special ingredients to make a New York bagel, Yum Yung. My sweet rice cakes are made with rice, sugar, and water. This bagel calls for flour, sea salt, and honey."

Yum Yung jumped. "Did you say flour, sea salt, and honey?"

"Yes," Baker Oh replied.

"I will return!" Yum Yung promised.

And indeed he did return—with Farmer Ahn and Fisherman Kee and Beekeeper Lee.

"I have the flour!" exclaimed Farmer Ahn.

"I have the sea salt!" exclaimed Fisherman Kee.

"And I have the honey!" exclaimed Beekeeper Lee.

124

It was time to make a New York bagel!

Baker Oh tied an apron around Yum Yung's waist. Following the recipe, Yum Yung instructed Farmer Ahn to sift flour into a mixing bowl. He instructed Fisherman Kee to sprinkle in the sea salt. He instructed Beekeeper Lee to spoon in the golden honey. Then Baker Oh poured in the water and tossed in a pinch of yeast.

Yum Yung kneaded the fragrant dough and formed it into a ring shape. He perfected the edges, especially for the hole in the middle. He dropped the dough into a large pot of simmering water. Minutes later, it floated to the top.

Then Yum Yung sprinkled it with sesame seeds, and into the oven it went.

Yum Yung watched the dough magically puff higher and higher until it nearly filled the whole oven—until it was a golden brown bagel!

The bagel was so big that Farmer Ahn, Fisherman Kee, Beekeeper Lee, and Baker Oh had to help Yum Yung carry it out of Oh's Heavenly Bakery. They all grunted as they set the bagel down under a persimmon tree on the quiet hillside. Yum Yung broke off a piece of the bagel for each of his friends.

"Hmm!" said Farmer Ahn.

"Oh!" said Fisherman Kee.

"Ah!" said Beekeeper Lee.

"Mmm!" said Baker Oh.

127

The moment had finally come for Yum Yung to eat his New York bagel.

He closed his eyes and took his first bite. It was a perfect bagel with a hint of honey so sweet it made him sigh. It was soft and plump and chewy and delicious all in one bite. It was so heavenly he could even taste the curious hole in the middle!

Yum Yung declared:

"At last I have my bagel!"

128

Turn and Talk

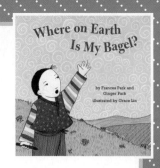

Where on Earth Is My Bagel?

by Frances Park and Ginger Park
illustrated by Grace Lin

Use details from *Where on Earth Is My Bagel?* to answer these questions with a partner.

1. **Make Inferences** Yum Yung decides that his bagel must be lost. What does he do next? What does that tell you about Yum Yung?

2. What is the setting? How is the setting important to the story events?

3. How do the people in Yum Yung's community work together to solve his problem?

Talking Tip

Complete the sentence to ask your partner for more information about an answer.

Could you tell me more about _____?

Write a Story

PROMPT How would the pigeon tell the story? How is the pigeon's point of view different from the other characters'? Use details from the words and pictures to explain your ideas.

PLAN First, draw or write what happens first, next, and last from the pigeon's point of view.

First

Next

Last

WRITE Now write the pigeon's version of the story. Include details that tell what the pigeon sees, does, hears, and feels. Remember to:

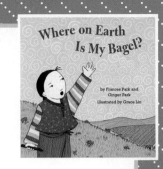

- Tell the story events in order.

- Use the words *I* and *me* to write in the pigeon's voice.

_____

_____

_____

_____

_____

_____

_____

_____

_____

_____

Prepare to Read

GENRE STUDY **Realistic fiction** stories are made up but could happen in real life.

MAKE A PREDICTION Preview "A World of Art." A second-grade class is going to an art museum. What do you think they will see?

_____

_____

_____

_____

_____

_____

SET A PURPOSE Read to find out what happens on the field trip to the museum.

A World of Art

READ How does Mr. Lyons feel about art? How can you tell?

Today, my class took a field trip to an art museum! Mr. Lyons, our teacher, said that creating art is one way people can share their culture. At the museum, Mr. Lyons showed us a mask from Africa that was carved from wood.

"Look at this amazing mask, kids," Mr. Lyons said. "Masks are one part of African culture. Food, clothes, art, music, and beliefs are all parts of a group's culture. Look closely. What does this mask remind you of?"

"I think it's a cat," I said.

Close Reading Tip
Circle words you don't know. Then figure them out.

READ What are alebrijes? <u>Underline</u> clues that tell you.

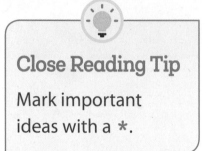

Close Reading Tip

Mark important ideas with a *.

Next, we looked at art from Mexico called alebrijes. Mr. Lyons told us these sculptures of animals are always painted bright colors because bright colors are part of everyday life in Mexico. I saw a pretty carving of an elephant with butterfly wings! Then Mr. Lyons pointed to a bright green panther. When he asked what it reminded us of, Marcus and I both said "A cat!" at the exact same time. Then we started laughing.

Finally, Mr. Lyons asked if every piece of art is the same. We all said "No way!" at the same time. Mr. Lyons smiled and said, "Every piece of art is different and special in its own way. That makes it unique, just like every person is unique."

CHECK MY UNDERSTANDING

What lesson does Mr. Lyons want the kids to learn?

_____

_____

_____

WRITE ABOUT IT What did you learn about African masks and Mexican alebrijes? Use your own words.

_____

_____

_____

_____

_____

_____

_____

_____

_____

_____

USA England Sweden

Prepare to Read

GENRE STUDY **Narrative nonfiction** gives facts about a topic, but it reads like a story. As you read *May Day Around the World*, pay attention to:

- main topic and details
- real settings
- dialogue, or what the characters in the story say

SET A PURPOSE Make a good guess, or **prediction,** about what the text will be about. Use the text features, like headings, to help you predict. Read to see if you are right. If not, make a new prediction.

POWER WORDS
trunk
races
clutched
forgot

Build Background: May Day

Hawaii
USA France

May Day

Around the World

by Tori Telfer

illustrated by Lynne Avril

SWEDEN

Uppsala, Sweden

Gustaf has never been up this late! He watches his father throw another piece of old furniture on the bonfire. Tonight they are celebrating Walpurgis Eve, the last day before spring.

Gustaf's neighbors sing soft songs around the fire. His mother brings him a green blanket and a bowl of nettle soup. "Spring is coming in the morning," she whispers.

Gustaf curls up on the blanket and feels the lovely

Austin, TX, USA

Maria and Carlos put a May Day basket on Ms. Garcia's doorstep. The basket is filled with purple violets and a chocolate bar.

Maria rings the doorbell, and they run behind a big oak tree. *Creak!* The door is opening!

Maria peeks out from behind the trunk. "Happy May Day, Ms. Garcia!"

139

Paris, France

Adèle races through the park with a coin clutched in her hand. May Day is her favorite time of year. Everyone is wearing bright colors, and the birds are just starting to sing.

"One lily of the valley, *s'il vous plaît*," she says to the man selling flowers.

Adèle runs back to her grandfather and puts the flower in his buttonhole. "*Joyeux premier mai, Papi!*" she says.

"Happy May Day, Grandpa!"

140

Wailea, Hawaii, USA

A'ala helps her aunt Malia get ready for the Lei Day parade. Her aunt has been crowned Lei Queen!

"How do I look?" asks her aunt.

"You forgot something," says A'ala. She slips a long, delicate lei of ilima blossoms over her aunt's head. The lei smells sweet and fresh, just like springtime.

"Now *you* forgot something!" says her aunt Malia. "Giving a lei means you get a kiss."

141

Peasmarsh, England

Annabelle and Edward are dancing around the Maypole. They've been practicing for weeks! If they get the steps just right, the ribbons will wind around the pole in a beautiful crisscross pattern. Annabelle wears her new white dress and yellow ribbon in her hair, the color of the first spring daisies. Edward is dressed as "The Green Man," full of mischief.

Oh, no! Edward's dog, Sammy, is running toward the Maypole. He wants to dance, too!

Watch out, Edward!

Turn and Talk

Use details from *May Day Around the World* to answer these questions with a partner.

1. **Make and Confirm Predictions** How did using the headings and other text features help you make predictions before and as you read? What were you right about? What was different?

2. Compare two of the May Day celebrations. How are they alike and different?

3. What was the author's purpose for writing this text?

Listening Tip

Look at your partner. Listen politely and find out what your partner is saying.

Write a Description

PROMPT If you could go to one celebration from *May Day Around the World*, which one would you choose? What would it be like? Use details from the text and illustrations to explain your ideas.

PLAN First, fill in the web with four details about the holiday.

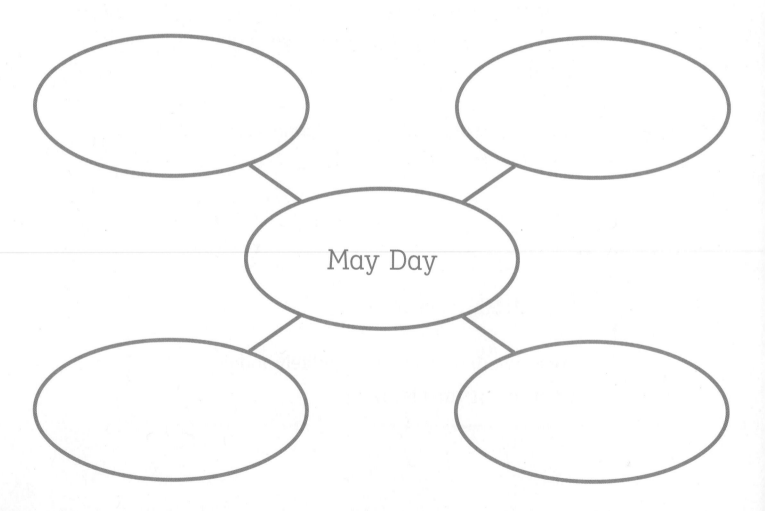

May Day

WRITE Now, write a description of the May Day celebration you would like to attend. Tell what you would see, hear, taste, and do. Remember to:

- Use words that paint a picture of the celebration.

- Capitalize the name of the holiday.

_____

_____

_____

_____

_____

_____

_____

_____

_____

Prepare to Read

GENRE STUDY **Narrative nonfiction** gives facts about a topic, but it reads like a story.

MAKE A PREDICTION Preview "Happy New Year!" You know that narrative nonfiction includes facts and details about a real topic. What do you think you will read about in this text?

_____

_____

_____

_____

_____

_____

SET A PURPOSE Read to learn how one family celebrates the start of a new year.

Happy New Year!

READ What predictions did you make before reading? Which facts in the text cause you to change your predictions?

My family lives in New York City. It's December 31 and we are celebrating New Year's Eve. My sister Alexa and I are wearing silly hats and blowing on noisemakers. Outside our window, people are gathered outside to celebrate together. It is loud and exciting.

Mom and Dad say we can stay up late. Right before midnight, the crowd outside our windows will begin counting down the last seconds of the year. "10, 9, 8, …" At midnight, everyone will shout, "Happy New Year!" Colorful confetti will fall all around the crowd. ▶

Close Reading Tip

Mark the topic with *.

READ Which details tell what the celebration looks like? <u>Underline</u> them.

Close Reading Tip

Put a **?** by the parts you have questions about.

Now, it is February. We are celebrating Chinese New Year. Our house is decorated with red lanterns. Dad explains that Chinese New Year is a celebration that spring is coming. Today, we are going to Chinatown for the celebration.

We will hear thousands of firecrackers. Bright streamers will fly, and we will see traditional dancers dressed in bright colors. Later, we will watch the parade. Lion dancers rear up on their hind legs and twirl. Finally, the long, colorful dragon weaves its way down the street. Everyone is cheering and having fun. What a happy new year!

CHECK MY UNDERSTANDING

What is the central idea of the text?

_____

_____

_____

WRITE ABOUT IT Compare the two New Year's celebrations.
How are they the same? How are they different? Use details from
the text in your answer.

_____

_____

_____

_____

_____

_____

_____

_____

_____

_____

Prepare to Read

> **GENRE STUDY** **Informational text** is nonfiction. It gives facts about a topic. As you read *Goal!*, pay attention to:

- details and facts about a topic
- facts about the world
- photographs

> **SET A PURPOSE** Read to find out the most important ideas in each part. Then **synthesize,** or put together these ideas in your mind, to find out what the text really means to you.

Meet Sean Taylor.

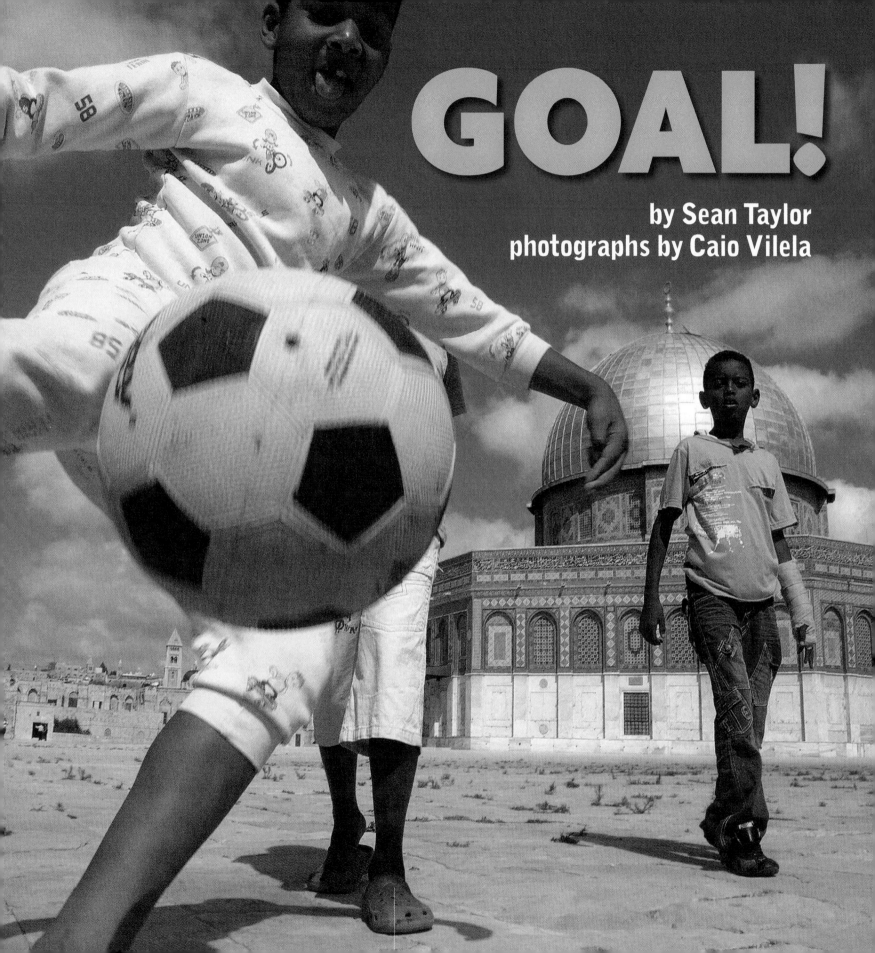

GOAL!

by Sean Taylor
photographs by Caio Vilela

Where there's a ball, there will always be someone who wants to play soccer.

Brazil

U.S.A.

When you play soccer, you're not allowed to use your arms and hands unless you are the goalkeeper.

But you can use the rest of your body—your feet, your legs, your hips, your chest, and your head.

152

There are more than 6,000 different languages spoken on our planet. But children all over the world understand soccer.

In some sports, teams can score up to 100 points in a game. In a soccer game you don't get many goals. Sometimes you don't get any at all. You have to be patient. So when a goal comes, it's special!

Spain

153

England

When the ball comes your way, you might feel excited, you might feel calm, you might even feel a bit scared.

Playing soccer teaches you lots of things—how to be quick, how to be clever, how to see what's going on around you, and how to be brave.

You can play soccer almost anywhere—in a garden, down an alley, on a playground, in a park, or on a beach.

You don't need to buy anything to play soccer. You can make goalposts with two stones, two sticks, or two shirts.

If you don't have a real soccer ball, you can make one with rolled-up socks, newspaper, and string, or even an orange in a plastic bag.

Some people invent machines. Some people invent medicines. And some people invent tricks with soccer balls.

When you trick a defender by pretending to go one way and then send the player after an imaginary ball, it's called a step-over. When you throw yourself in the air and kick the ball over your head, it's called a bicycle kick.

Jordan

Iran

Every soccer game is like a story. It's full of characters, emotions, and drama.

And no one knows how it will end until the **final** whistle blows.

There's nothing quite like the excitement before you start a game of soccer. Anything can happen!

At the end of the game, you may have won or you may have lost. But you can lose a game and still play your very best. And that is a kind of winning.

Pakistan

Nepal

Soccer is not about showing off how well you can play.
It's about showing how well you can play for your team.
The best players don't worry about being the stars of
their teams. They want their teams to be the stars.

The ball doesn't care if you're big or small. It doesn't care what your religion is, what race you are, or where you come from. It doesn't even care if you're good at soccer.

Anyone can play soccer—anywhere in the world.

You can have fun playing soccer with just one friend or even on your own.

China

New Zealand

No other sport brings people together like soccer. No other sport is played by so many people in so many different countries. When you are playing soccer, there will always be someone else playing, somewhere in the world.

Soccer Around the World

Soccer is played all over the world! And in most other countries—except Canada and the U.S.A.—it is called football.

Here are the countries mentioned in this book and the year each country's first national soccer team was founded.

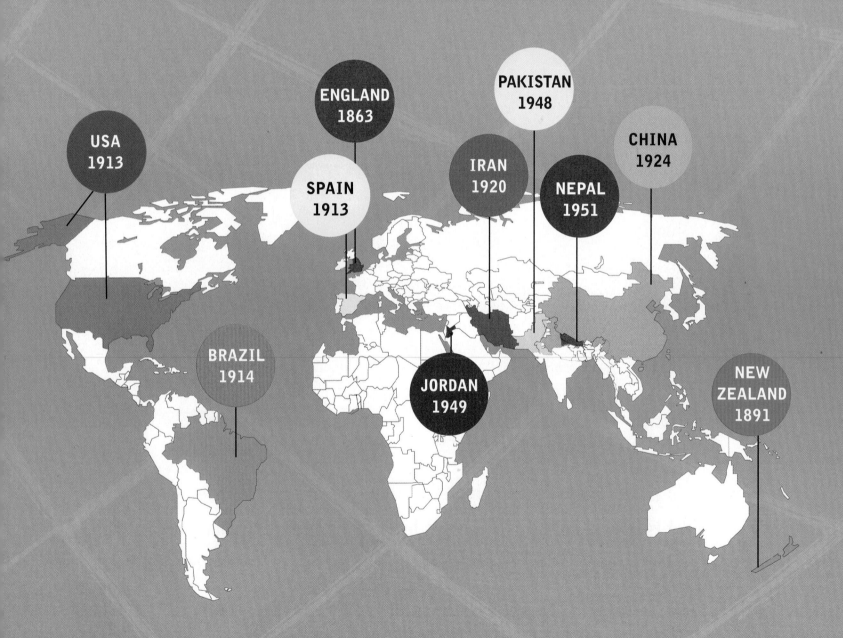

USA 1913

ENGLAND 1863

PAKISTAN 1948

CHINA 1924

SPAIN 1913

IRAN 1920

NEPAL 1951

BRAZIL 1914

JORDAN 1949

NEW ZEALAND 1891

GOAL!
by Sean Taylor
photographs by Caio Vilela

Use details from *Goal!* to answer these questions with a partner.

1. **Synthesize** Why do you think that soccer is loved all
   around the world?

2. Look back at pages 158–159. What is the main idea of this
   section? What does the author want readers to understand
   about soccer?

3. How can you use the map on page 160 to find and
   understand information about soccer?

Talking Tip

Wait for your turn to speak. Tell about your
feelings and ideas clearly.

I feel that _____.

Write an Opinion

PROMPT What do you think it takes to be a great soccer player? Use details in the words and photographs to explain your ideas.

PLAN First, think of qualities a person would need to be a great soccer player. Write or draw them below.

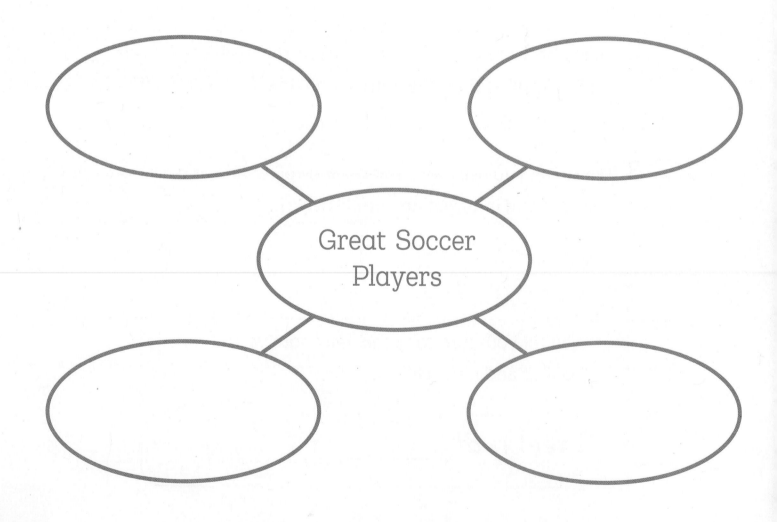

Great Soccer Players

WRITE Now write your opinion. Tell what qualities you think a person should have to be a great soccer player. Remember to:

- Be sure to explain your opinion with reasons.

- Include details that support your reasons.

_____

_____

_____

_____

_____

_____

_____

_____

_____

_____

Prepare to Read

GENRE STUDY **Informational text** is nonfiction. It gives facts about a topic.

MAKE A PREDICTION Preview "Time for School!" Most children around the world go to school. What do you think you will learn about schools?

_____

_____

_____

_____

_____

_____

_____

SET A PURPOSE Read to learn about schools around the world.

Time for School!

READ How do students get to school? <u>Underline</u> three ways.

Each day, kids all around the world go to school. How do they get there? In South Africa, many kids walk to school. In the Philippines, some kids ride in a yellow boat! In the United States, some kids take a yellow school bus. Some kids can go to school right inside their homes. Near or far, walk or ride, when kids get to school, they all do the same thing—they learn!

Close Reading Tip
Write C when you make a connection.

CHECK MY UNDERSTANDING

What is the most important idea on this page?

_____

_____

_____

165

READ Which details are most important? Mark them with a *.

Close Reading Tip

<u>Underline</u> a sentence that tells the author's opinion.

When does your school day begin and end? In Brazil, some schools begin at 7 o'clock in the morning and end at noon so that students can go home to have lunch with their families. In China, some schools begin at 7:30 in the morning and end at 5 o'clock in the afternoon.

I think it would be fun to visit schools all around the world! We would observe students conducting science experiments, learning new languages, creating art and music, and having fun together. Schools may have differences, but they have one thing in common. No matter where they are, no matter how and when kids get there, schools are a place for kids to learn and grow.

CHECK MY UNDERSTANDING

What is the central idea of the text?

_____

_____

_____

WRITE ABOUT IT Why is going to school an important part of life for kids all around the world? Use details from the text and from your experiences to explain your ideas.

_____

_____

_____

_____

_____

_____

_____

_____

_____

_____

Prepare to Read

GENRE STUDY **Poetry** uses images, sounds, and rhythm to express feelings. As you read *Poems in the Attic*, look at:

- how the poem makes you feel
- patterns of sounds, words, or lines
- words that appeal to the senses

SET A PURPOSE As you read, **make connections** by finding ways that this text is like things in your life and other texts you have read. This will help you understand and remember the text.

POWER WORDS

stacked

flitting

leave

breathless

mound

shuffled

clamber

adventures

Meet Nikki Grimes.

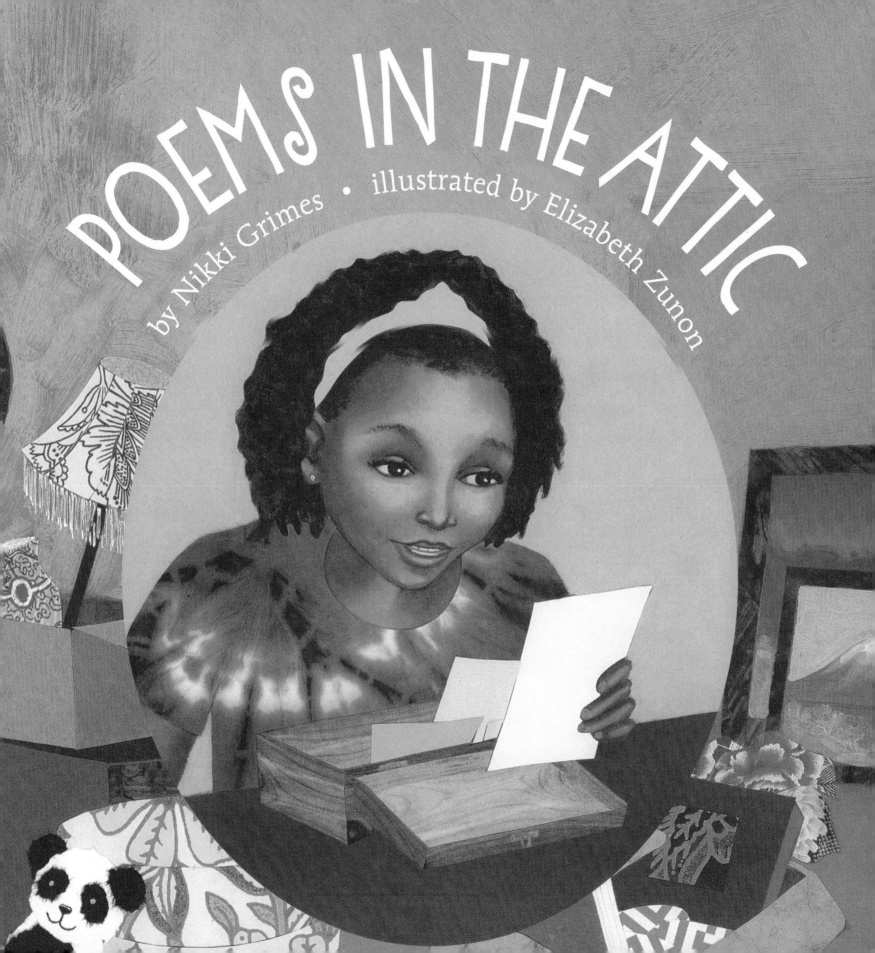

POEMS IN THE ATTIC

by Nikki Grimes • illustrated by Elizabeth Zunon

Poems in the Attic

Grandma's attic is stacked with secrets.
Last visit, I found poems Mama wrote
before I was born, before I was even imagined.
She started when she was seven—same age as me!

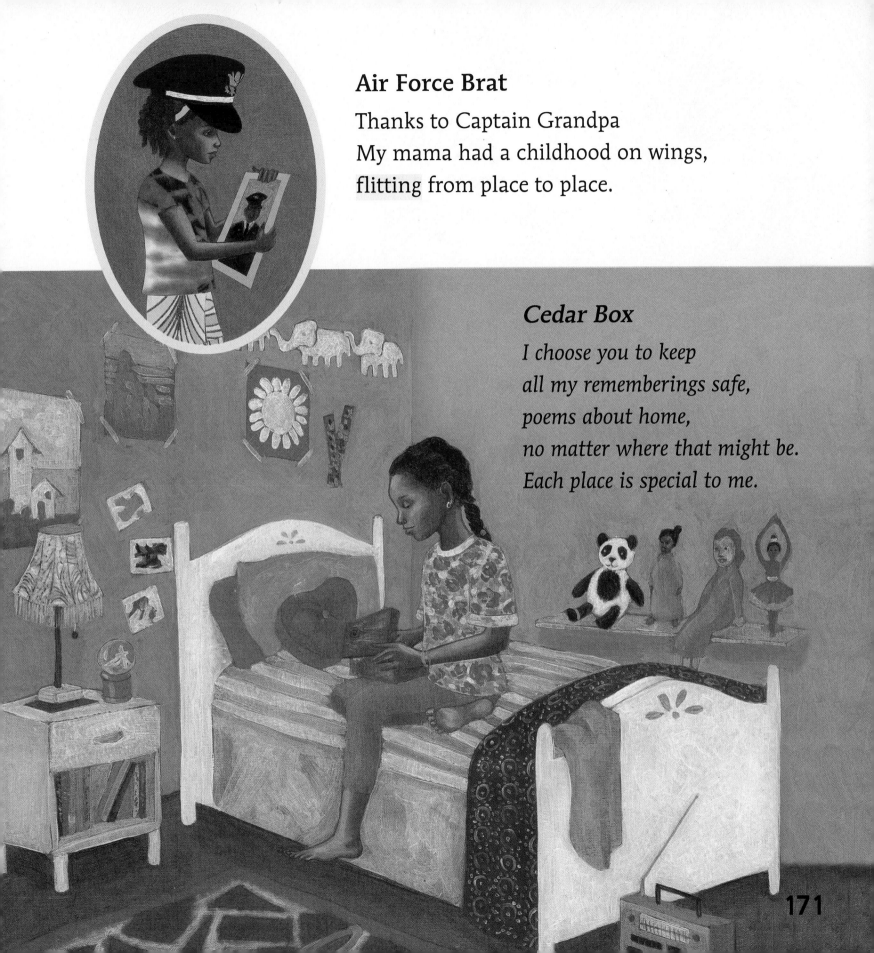

Air Force Brat

Thanks to Captain Grandpa
My mama had a childhood on wings,
flitting from place to place.

Cedar Box

*I choose you to keep
all my rememberings safe,
poems about home,
no matter where that might be.
Each place is special to me.*

171

Grandma Says

Memories can be like sandcastles
the waves wash away.
My mama glued her memories with words
so they would last forever.

Cabrillo Beach
CALIFORNIA

Home on leave, Daddy
took me to the Grunion Run!
Our flashlights found them—
slim fish, silver as new dimes,
wiggling ashore to lay eggs.

Bedtime

Grandma sings me to sleep
with one of Mama's poems.
I dream of skies
my mother's eyes have seen.

Aurora Borealis
ALASKA

My brother and me
held hands, breathless, as we watched
this dancing rainbow
shimmy 'cross Alaska's sky
in a skirt of night and light.

173

Paper Candleholders

Next day, Grandma lays out paper bags,
scissors, and paint, teaching me
a kind of magic she and Mama used to make
every December, in New Mexico.

Luminarias
NEW MEXICO

I scalloped the tops,
Mom painted happy faces.
After we were done,
our brown bag candleholders
bloomed bright, lighting up the night.

Who Is She?

It's funny to think of Mama
making a mess with arts and crafts
or playing, sand in her hair,
giggling like a kid—like me!

White Sands National Monument
NEW MEXICO

I scaled the first dune,
brother close behind. On three,
we rolled down the mound,
tumbling in sand and laughter,
ready to do it again.

175

Snow Dream

I flip through old photos of Mama,
smile at the snowman that stands
taller than she. I never get to see
snow where we live.

Colorado Springs

COLORADO

Dad came home with skis
short as my little-girl legs.
I strapped them on tight,
shuffled across the backyard,
flying downhill—in my dreams.

Imagine

Three days of not seeing my mama
feels like forever.
I bet she used to miss her dad,
gone for months.

Garden of the Gods
COLORADO

On Bring Your Dad Day,
I brought along a photo
of the two of us
at the Garden of the Gods.
I clutched my photo, wishing . . . .

177

Boys

Guys at school tease me
for collecting rocks "like a boy."
Next time, I'll tell them to
gather sharks' teeth "like a girl"!

Cherry Point
NORTH CAROLINA

Any day's perfect
for walking the river's edge.
I slipped over rocks,
gathered bruises and sharks' teeth
to show Dad when he's on leave.

178

Sailing

Pictures of kayaks and canoes
swim on the blue of our walls
thanks to Mama, who buys them all.
Now I think I know why.

Accotink Bay
VIRGINIA

The bay called us three.
We silently kayaked near
the bird-breeding box.
If only Dad would let us
clamber atop it and dance!

179

City Slicker

We've lived in the city
long as I can remember,
but Mama is always going on about
nature and the wonders of the woods.

Brackenridge Park

TEXAS

Dad says I'm lucky.
Mom sent me horseback riding
in the morning mist,
and as it cleared, I spotted
a great, green heron lift, soar!

Chopsticks

At dinner I ask Grandma
for the chopsticks Mama
taught me to use. Once, I asked Mama
where she learned, and she just smiled.

Cherry Blossoms
JAPAN

Spring! Kimono time.
I joined the parade of girls
strolling avenues
dusted with cherry blossoms.
I caught a few, like snowflakes.

Tent

I set up a tent
in Grandma's backyard,
take a flashlight so I can read.
Mama's poems and me go camping.

Class Trip

JAPAN

My class camping trip!
Rhinoceros beetles and
dragonflies joined us.
We ate squid-on-a-stick, slept
at the foot of Mount Fuji.

182

Moving Day

I don't know how she did it,
moving all the time.
I get dizzy thinking about
all those good-byes.

Station Next

PORTUGAL

Move Number—who knows?
We call them all adventures.
I pack my poems,
wishing I could fold my friends
and slip them in my suitcase.

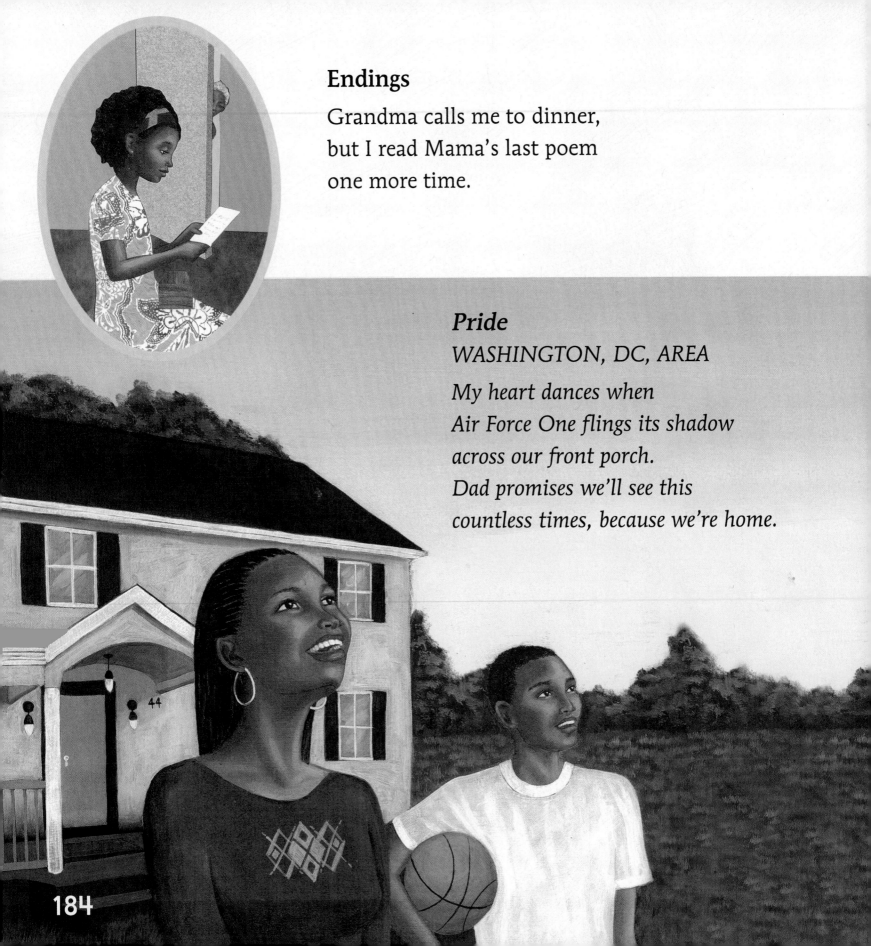

Endings

Grandma calls me to dinner,
but I read Mama's last poem
one more time.

Pride

WASHINGTON, DC, AREA

My heart dances when
Air Force One flings its shadow
across our front porch.
Dad promises we'll see this
countless times, because we're home.

Time to Go

Mama comes for me tomorrow.
I have a surprise for her.
I've been busy writing
poems of my own.

Let's See

Pencil and paper,
hole punch and ribbon—all set.
I work past bedtime,
copy Mama's poems, then
stitch them together with mine.

185

Back to the Attic

I put Mama's poems back in the chest
where I found them
and leave a stack of mine
for someone else to find.

The Gift

I run to Mama,
tackle her with hugs, kisses,
then hand her the book.
Breathlessly, I wait for her
to unwrap our memories.

Use details from *Poems in the Attic* to answer these questions with a partner.

1. **Make Connections** Describe a time you visited somewhere you had never been before. How does that experience help you understand the characters in this text?

2. What does the girl mean when she says, "I dream of skies my mother's eyes have seen"?

3. These poems tell two stories. Who is the narrator of each story? How are their stories alike and different?

Listening Tip

You learn from others by listening carefully. Think about what your partner says and what you learn.

Write a Memory Poem

PROMPT The main character says that her mama glued her memories with words so they would last forever. Think of a memory you would like to remember forever. How would you describe it in a poem?

PLAN First, make a chart. On one side, write details about your special memory. On the other side, write words with interesting sounds that describe each detail. Look back at the text for ideas.

Details	Words

WRITE Now write your poem using the best words on your chart. Remember to:

- Use words that paint a picture of your topic.

- Think about how the words in your poem sound together.

_____

_____

_____

_____

_____

_____

_____

_____

_____

_____

Prepare to Read

GENRE STUDY **Poetry** uses images, sounds, and rhythm to express feelings.

MAKE A PREDICTION Preview "Something to Share." Jay forgot to bring something to share on Celebrating Cultures Day at school. What do you think he will do?

_____

_____

_____

_____

_____

_____

_____

SET A PURPOSE Read to find out if Jay solves his problem.

Something to Share

READLET How would you feel if you were Jay?

On Celebrating Cultures Day, in the grade 2 class,

Most kids were feeling happy, but Jay Patel, alas!

He had forgotten to bring in something he could share.

The teacher, alphabetically, called out each child's name.

Lisa Barton taught the class to play a Russian game.

Alma Green used paper plates to make a special mask.

> **Close Reading Tip**
> Write C when you make a connection.

CHECK MY UNDERSTANDING

What problem does Jay have at the beginning of the poem?

_____

_____

_____

191

READ How does Jay feel while waiting for his turn? <u>Underline</u> the clues that tell you.

Close Reading Tip

<u>Underline</u> the sentence that tells how Jay's mom helps him. Was your prediction about the problem and resolution correct? What was different?

Dan Jens played a Hopi flute, a lovely little tune.

But Jay Patel was worried. His turn was coming soon.

Everyone said "Hurray!" when Pete Orr gave out pizza.

"Jay Patel," the teacher called. The moment was now here.

In the front, Jay shuffled, sighed, and fidgeted in fear.

Then, it came. In his mind, Jay saw his mother's yoga.

Jay said, "Time for tree pose. Get up out of your chair!

Balance on one leg and put your arms up in the air!"

Jay thought, "Thanks to Mom, I had something cool to share!"

CHECK MY UNDERSTANDING

How does Jay solve his problem?

_____

_____

_____

_____

WRITE ABOUT IT What happens in the beginning, middle, and end of the poem? Retell the main events in your own words.

_____

_____

_____

_____

_____

_____

_____

_____

_____

_____

Prepare to View

GENRE STUDY **Videos** are short movies that give you information or something for you to watch for enjoyment. As you watch *What's for Lunch Around the World?*, notice:

- how pictures, sounds, and words work together
- information about the topic
- the purpose of the video

SET A PURPOSE Some videos use **graphic features** in the same way that print books do. As you view, think about how these features help you find information quickly in the video.

Build Background: Favorite Foods

What's for Lunch Around the World?

As You View Discover what's for lunch today! Look carefully at the pictures. Watch for the labels that pop up. How do the words and pictures work together to show you what people all around the world eat for lunch?

What's for Lunch Around the World?

Turn and Talk

Use details from *What's for Lunch Around the World?* to answer these questions with a partner.

1. **Graphic Features** How can you use the labels to understand more about each lunch?

2. What are some things that the lunches have in common?

3. Which of the lunches would you most like to eat? Which food are you most curious to try? Use details from the video to explain your opinions.

Talking Tip

Add your own idea to what your partner says. Be sure to be polite.

I like your idea. My idea is _____.

Let's Wrap Up!

? Essential Question

What can we learn from different people and cultures?

Pick one of these activities to show what you have learned about the topic.

1. Why Study Cultures?

Write a paragraph to explain why it is important to learn about people and traditions from different parts of the world. Use details from the texts to explain your opinion.

Word Challenge

Can you use the word harmony in your opinion?

2. Collage of Cultures!

Think about the texts you read. What do they teach you about how people share their cultures with others? Draw or find pictures that show what you've learned. Then make a collage. Add labels to describe your pictures. Share your collage with a partner.

My Notes

Glossary

adventures

arrive

A

adventures [ăd-věn′chərz]   **Adventures** are exciting experiences.

We have many fun **adventures** together.

arrive [ə-rīv′]   When you **arrive**, you get to a place. Grandma and Grandpa were very happy to see us **arrive** for a visit.

attached [ə-tăcht′]   When things are **attached**, they are joined together.

These papers are **attached** with a staple.

B

breathless [brĕth′lĭs]   If you are **breathless**, you have a hard time catching your breath.

I was **breathless** after running up the hill.

C

clamber [klăm'bər, klăm'ər]   When you **clamber**, you climb quickly using your hands and feet.
We **clamber** up the rocks to reach the top.

clutched [klŭcht]   If you **clutched** something, you held it tightly.
Tyler **clutched** his father's hand.

coast [kōst]   The **coast** is the land that is next to the sea.
We love walking along the **coast**.

crack [krăk]   **Crack** means to break or split.
You have to **crack** the coconut open to eat it.

crouches [krouch'ĭz]   When something **crouches**, it bends its legs and lowers its body.
The tiger **crouches** in the tall grass.

clutched

coast

culture [kŭl′chər] A group's **culture** is the ideas and beliefs the people share.
Making this special meal together is an important part of my family's **culture**.

delight

D

darting [därt′ĭng] If something is **darting**, it is moving from place to place very quickly.
We saw a deer **darting** across the street.

delight [dĭ-līt′] **Delight** is great joy.
Being together filled us all with **delight**.

E

ecosystem [ē′kō-sĭs′təm, ēk′ō-sĭs′təm] An **ecosystem** is all the animals and plants that live in the same area.
A pond is one type of **ecosystem**.

ecosystem

F

final [fī′nəl]   In a group of events, the **final** one is the last one.
Today is the **final** day of the sale.

flitting [flĭt′ĭng]   If you are **flitting**, you are moving quickly from place to place.
Two birds were **flitting** from tree to tree.

flock [flŏk]   A **flock** is a group of birds.
We saw a **flock** of geese in the pond.

flock

forgot [fər-gŏt′, fôr-gŏt′]   If you **forgot** something, you did not remember it.
I **forgot** to pack my homework.

founded [found′ĭd]   The date when something was **founded** was when it was started or created.
The camp was **founded** five years ago.

fragrant [frā′grənt]   Something **fragrant** smells sweet.
I smelled the **fragrant** flowers.

forgot

G

growled [grould]   If something **growled**, it made a deep, angry sound.
My stomach **growled** before lunch.

grumpy

grumpy [grŭm'pē]   Someone who is **grumpy** is in a bad mood.
Val was **grumpy** because she missed her favorite show.

grunted [grŭnt'ĭd]   If you **grunted**, you made a low, deep sound.
He **grunted** as he tried to lift the heavy chair.

H

habitat

habitat [hăb'ĭ-tăt']   A **habitat** is a place where plants and animals live and grow.
We saw an elephant in its natural **habitat**.

harmony [här'mə-nē]   Being in **harmony** means living together in a peaceful way.
My family lives in **harmony** together.

heritage [hĕr′ĭ-tĭj]   A country's **heritage** is its way of doing things that is passed down over time.
We learned about our family **heritage** from Grandpa.

hide [hīd]   A **hide** is an animal's skin.
The shoes are made of animal **hide**.

hollered [hŏl′ərd]   If you **hollered**, you shouted loudly.
We **hollered** as loudly as we could.

hollered

I

imaginary [ĭ-măj′ə-nĕr′ē]   Something that is **imaginary** only happens in your mind.
He wrote a story about an **imaginary** world with talking animals.

J

joking [jōk′ĭng]   If you are **joking**, you are saying something to be funny.
I was **joking** with my friends at the slumber party.

joking

205

leave

L

leave [lēv]   A **leave** is time away from work.
I am so happy that my father is home on **leave** now.

M

mingles [mĭng'gəlz]   When something **mingles** with another thing, the two things mix together.
The new camper **mingles** with other children at camp.

mound [mound]   A **mound** is a hill or pile.
There was a **mound** of dirt next to the house while it was under construction.

mound

N

nod [nŏd]   A **nod** is when you move your head up and down to show that you agree.
She gave me a **nod** and kept talking.

O

offered [ô'fərd, ŏf'ərd]   If you **offered** something to someone, you asked to give it to him or her.
She **offered** her teacher an apple.

offered

P

patient [pā'shənt]   If you are **patient**, you can wait for something without complaining.
I am **patient** with my baby brother.

prances [prăns'ĭz]   When something **prances**, it moves by taking high steps.
The beautiful horse **prances** in the snow.

R

races [rās'ĭz]   Someone who **races** runs or moves very fast.
She **races** outside to catch the bus.

prances

route

route [roōt, rout]   A **route** is the path someone takes to get from place to place.

We will take the quickest **route** to the concert hall for the big show.

S

sheltered [shĕl'tərd]   A **sheltered** place protects from wind and rain.

The cave was a **sheltered** place.

sheltered

shrugged [shrŭgd]   If you **shrugged**, you lifted and lowered your shoulders to show you did not know.

He **shrugged** his shoulders when I asked if he thought it would rain.

shuffled [shŭf'əld]   If you **shuffled**, you walked slowly and dragged your feet.

I heard crunching sounds as I **shuffled** through the fallen leaves.

slippery [slĭp'ə-rē]   Something **slippery** is wet, smooth, and hard to hold.

The road was **slippery** after the rain.

smothered [smŭ*th*'ərd]   Something that is **smothered** is thickly covered with something else.

The delicious toast was **smothered** with butter and strawberry jam.

species [spē'shēz, spē'sēz]   A **species** is a group of animals or plants that are alike.

The nature center had many **species** of frogs.

stacked [stăkt]   If you **stacked** things, you placed them on top of other things.

I **stacked** the boxes in the garage.

stacked

stubborn [stŭb'ərn]   Someone who is **stubborn** does not want to change.

My cousin is **stubborn** and will not change his mind.

surface [sûr'fəs]   The **surface** of something is the top or outside of it.

The beautiful fish swam up to the **surface** of the pond to be fed.

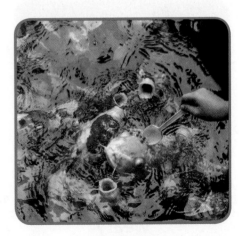

surface

209

trills

T

trills [trĭlz]   When a bird **trills**, it sings and chirps.
The bird **trills** near my window.

trunk [trŭngk]   A **trunk** is the main part of a tree from which branches grow.
The very old tree had a huge **trunk** that many of us could hide behind.

tucked [tŭkt]   If you **tucked** something, you pushed it behind or into something else.
He **tucked** his shirt into his pants.

W

weary

weary [wîr′ē]   Someone who is **weary** is very tired.
We were all beginning to feel **weary** as we got closer to the finish line.

wit [wĭt]   **Wit** is a talent for using words to be funny.
These books are full of **wit**.

wobbly [wŏb′lē]   Something that is **wobbly** is moving from side to side in a shaky way.

The newborn donkey was **wobbly** on his feet.

wraps [răps]   If something **wraps** around another thing, it winds or goes around that thing.

He **wraps** a blanket around himself to keep warm.

wobbly

211

Index of Titles and Authors

Acknowledgments

Abuelo and the Three Bears/Abuelo y los tres osos by Jerry Tello, illustrated by Ana López Escrivá. Text copyright ©1997 by Jerry Tello. Illustrations copyright ©1997 by Ana López Escrivá. Reprinted by permission of Houghton Mifflin Harcourt Publishing Company.

"The Ant" from *Mamá Goose: A Latino Nursery Treasure* by Alma Flor Ada and F. Isabel Campoy. Text copyright © 2004 by Alma Flor Ada and F. Isabel Campoy. Reprinted by permission of Disney/ Hyperion Books, an imprint of Disney Publishing Worldwide, LLC.

"Big Brown Moose" from *Winter Bees & Other Poems of the Cold* by Joyce Sidman, illustrated by Rick Allen. Text copyright © 2014 by Joyce Sidman. Illustrations copyright © 2014 by Rick Allen. Reprinted by permission of Houghton Mifflin Harcourt Publishing Company.

"The Cricket" (retitled from "El Grillo") from *También los Insectos son Perfectos* by Alberto Blanco. Text copyright © 1993 by Alberto Blanco. Translated and reprinted by permission of CIDCLI.

Goal! by Sean Taylor, photos by Caio Vilela. Text copyright © 2014 by Sean Taylor. Photos copyright © 2012 by Caio Vilela. Reprinted by arrangement with Henry Holt Books for Young Readers and Frances Lincoln, Ltd.

The Long, Long Journey (retitled from *The Long, Long Journey: The Godwit's Amazing Migration*) by Sandra Markle, illustrated by Mia Posada. Text copyright © 2013 by Sandra Markle. Illustrations copyright © 2013 by Mia Posada. Reprinted with the permission of Millbrook Press, a division of Lerner Publishing Group, Inc.

"May Day Around the World" by Tori Telfer, illustrated by Lynne Avril from *Ladybug* Magazine, Volume 20 Issue 5, May/June 2010. Text copyright © 2010 by Carus Publishing Company. Reprinted by permission of Cricket Media. All Cricket Media material is copyrighted by Carus Publishing d/b/a Cricket Media, and/or various authors and illustrators. Any commercial use or distribution of material without permission is strictly prohibited. Please visit http://www.cricketmedia.com/info/licensing for licensing and http://www.cricketmedia.com for subscriptions.

Excerpts from *Poems in the Attic* by Nikki Grimes, illustrated by Elizabeth Zunon. Text copyright © 2015 by Nikki Grimes. Illustrations copyright © 2015 by Elizabeth Zunon. Reprinted by permission of Lee & Low Books Inc.

"Polar Bear Family" from *Polar Bear, Arctic Hare: Poems of the Frozen North* by Eileen Spinelli. Text copyright © 2007 by Eileen Spinelli. Published by WordSong, an imprint of Boyds Mills Press. Reprinted by permission of Boyds Mills Press.

Excerpt from *Sea Otter Pups* by Ruth Owen. Text copyright © 2013 by Bearport Publishing Company, Inc. Reprinted by permission of Bearport Publishing Company, Inc.

Excerpt from *The Tiny Caterpillar and the Great Big Tree* by Kelly Moran, illustrated by Lynne Lorbeske. Text copyright © 2009 by Kelly Moran. Reprinted by permission of Kelly Moran.

Where on Earth Is My Bagel? by Frances and Ginger Park, illustrated by Grace Lin. Text copyright © 2001 by Frances Park and Ginger Park. Illustrations copyright © 2001 by Grace Lin. Reprinted by permission of Lee & Low Books Inc.

Credits

4 (bg) ©Rina Oshi/Shutterstock, (bc) ©MariMarkina/iStock/Getty Images Plus/Getty Images; 4 (bl) ©Tom Middleton/Shutterstock; 4 (bl) (bg) ©moomsabuy/Shutterstock; 5 (b) ©Terra Mater Factual Studios; 7 (bl) (all) ©Houghton Mifflin Harcourt; 8 ©shikheigoh/RooM/Getty Images; 12 (c) ©Comodo777/Shutterstock; 13 (l) ©Rixipix/iStock/Getty Images Plus/Getty Images; 13 (c) ©Cloudtail_the_Snow_Leopard/iStock/Getty Images Plus/Getty Images; 13 (br) ©belizar/Shutterstock; 13 (tr) ©Olha Chernova/Shutterstock; 14 ©Casey Brooke/Houghton Mifflin Harcourt; 32 ©milehightraveler/iStock/Getty Images Plus/Getty Images; 33 ©milehightraveler/iStock/Getty Images Plus/Getty Images; 34 ©mlharing/iStock/Getty Images Plus/Getty Images; 36 ©Darryl Leniuk/Lifesize/Getty Images; 37 ©Tom Middleton/Shutterstock, ©moomsabuy/Shutterstock; 38 ©Milo Burcham/Design Pics/Getty Images; 39 ©Kevin Schafer/Corbis/Getty Images; 40 (b) ©Milo Burcham/Design Pics Inc./Alamy; 40 (t) ©Zoom Team/Fotolia; 40 (inset) ©Cosmographies; 41 ©Richard Mittleman/Gon2Foto/Alamy; 42 ©David Litman/Shutterstock; 43 (t) ©Angel Simon/Shutterstock; 43 (b) ©Roberta Olenick/All Canada Photos/Superstock; 44 ©Marcos Amend/Shutterstock; 44 (inset) ©PhotoviewPlus/Moment Open/Getty Images; 45 ©Sieto/iStock/Getty Images Plus; 46 ©Kirsten Wahlquist/Shutterstock; 47 ©Tom Middleton/Shutterstock, ©moomsabuy/Shutterstock; 49 ©Tom Middleton/Shutterstock, ©moomsabuy/Shutterstock; 54 ©Hu Zhao/Alamy; 72 ©AlexSuloev/iStock/Getty Images Plus/Getty Images; 96 ©Carol Polich Photo Workshops/Lonely Planet Images/Getty Images; 96 ©Terra Mater Factual Studios; 98 (b) ©Terra Mater Factual Studios; 99 (tr) ©Terra Mater Factual Studios; 100 ©Thanwan Singh Pannu/Shutterstock; 101 (r) ©Andresr/E+/Getty Images; 101 (l) ©kali9/iStock/Getty Images Plus/Getty Images; 102 ©Prisma by Dukas Presseagentur GmbH/Alamy; 108 (bl) ©Alan F. Bradley; 136 ©sarradet/iStock/Getty Images; 150 ©KT Bruce/KT Bruce Photography; 164 ©wavebreakmedia/Shutterstock; 166 ©wavebreakmedia/Shutterstock; 168 ©Lee & Low Books; 194 (all) ©Houghton Mifflin Harcourt; 194 (bl) (inset) ©Steve Debenport/iStock/Getty Images Plus/Getty Images; 195 (all) ©Houghton Mifflin Harcourt; 196 (b) ©Houghton Mifflin Harcourt; 197 (all) ©Houghton Mifflin Harcourt; 198 ©Getty Images; 199 ©kikovic/Shutterstock; 200 (b) ©Monkey Business Images/Shutterstock; 200 (t) ©PhotoLink/PhotoDisc/Getty Images; 201 (b) ©Cornelia Schaible/iStockPhoto.com; 201 (t) ©Photodisc/Getty Images; 202 (t) ©Jack Hollingsworth/Photodisc/Getty Images; 202 (b) ©Kazakova Maryia/Shutterstock; 203 (t) ©Jeremy Woodhouse/Photodisc/Getty Images; 203 (b) ©Mr. Nikon/Shutterstock; 204 (t) ©Photodisc/Getty Images; 204 (b) ©Quick Shot/Shutterstock; 205 (b) ©CREATISTA/Shutterstock; 205 (t) ©Digital Vision/Getty Images; 206 (b) ©Andrew F. Kazmierski/Shutterstock; 206 (t) ©Stockbyte/Getty Images; 207 (b) ©Rusla Ruseyn/Shutterstock; 207 (t) ©Rich Legg/iStockphoto.com; 208 (t) ©Maleo/Shutterstock; 208 (b) ©Marco Maccarini/iStock; 209 (b) ©Operation Shooting/Shutterstock; 209 (t) ©Sean Locke Photography/Shutterstock; 210 (t) ©Tim Zurowski/Shutterstock; 210 (b) ©Sam Dudgeon/HRW/Houghton Mifflin Harcourt; 211 ©risteski goce/Shutterstock